Griffith John

GRIFFITH JOHN

BY

JOHN AARON

EP BOOKS
1st Floor Venture House, 6 Silver Court, Watchmead,
Welwyn Garden City, UK, AL7 1TS

www.epbooks.org
sales@epbooks.org

EP BOOKS are distributed in the USA by:
JPL Fulfillment
3741 Linden Avenue Southeast,
Grand Rapids, MI 49548.

E-mail: sales@jplfulfillment.com
Tel: 877.683.6935

© John Aaron 2016. All rights reserved. No part of this publication may be reproduced, stored in a retrieval system or transmitted, in any form, or by any means, electronic, mechanical, photocopying, recording or otherwise, without the prior permission of the publishers.

First published 2016

ISBN 978–1–78397–151–0

British Library Cataloguing in Publication Data available

Contents

Timeline	7
Introduction	11
1. Childhood and youth in Swansea (1831–55)	13
2. Shanghai (1855–61)	21
3. First journeys during days of rebellion	25
4. The Opium Wars	31
5. Hankou (1861–70)—first steps	35
6. 'A perilous journey' (1866) and a visit home (1870)	43
7. Hankou—the years of service	49
8. Griffith John's priorities	55
9. A Time of Refreshing (1875)	65
10. The springboard to Central China (1871–85)	71
11. James Hudson Taylor and Timothy Richard	87
12. The Shanghai Missionary Conferences (1877, 1890 and 1907)	95
13. Home again (1880)	103
14. Revival, Hunan, and Revolution (1894–1900)	111
15. A death and a Jubilee (1905)	125
16. The last years (1902–12)	129
17. The forgotten missionary? How should Griffith John be remembered?	135
Further Reading	143

TIMELINE

1831	Griffith John born on 14 December
1832	Mother, Ann John, dies during a cholera epidemic
1839	Converted as an eight-year-old at Ebenezer Independent Church
1845	First experience of preaching, when only fourteen years old
1849	Father, also Griffith John, dies during a cholera epidemic. Elijah Jacob, his pastor, takes care of him
1850	Accepted at Brecon Theological College
1853	Accepted as a missionary by the London Missionary Society
1855	Ordained at Ebenezer; marries Margaret Griffiths; they sail for Shanghai, arriving 24 September
1850–64	Taiping Rebellion
1856–60	Second Opium War

1860	Treaty of Tientsin (Tianjin)
1861	John arrives at Hankou, Central China (now Wuhan) on 21 June
1862	First Protestant church in Central China constituted at Hankou
1866	John and Alexander Wylie sail a thousand miles up the Yangzi River
1866	First hospital built at Hankou
1870	Returns to Britain because of Margaret's ill-health
1873	Death of Margaret John at Singapore during return voyage to China
1874	John marries Jeannette Jenkins in September
1875	Hankou Tract Society (later Central China Religious Tract Society) established
1877	First Shanghai Missionary Conference, 10–24 May
1880	John in USA and then Britain because of Jeannette's ill-health
1885	John's translation of New Testament into Easy Wen-Li completed; Margaret John dies in December
1890	John's translation of New Testament into colloquial Mandarin completed; Second Shanghai Missionary Conference

Timeline

1895–96	Period of Revival in Hubei
1897	First Protestant baptisms in Hunan, the 'Last Province'
1899–1901	Boxer Uprising
1905	Death of Hudson Taylor, 4 June; Griffith John's Jubilee—50 years in China
1907	Third Shanghai Missionary Conference
1911	Retirement and final return to Britain
1912	Griffith John dies on 26 July in Clapton, London. He is buried at Sketty, Swansea

Introduction

Griffith John died in a nursing home in Clapton, London, over a hundred years ago, on 26 July 1912. *The Times* newspaper in its obituary column commented: 'We regret to record that Dr Griffith John, the great missionary in China, died yesterday afternoon.' A year previously, when reporting on his retirement from China, the Welsh daily newspaper, *The Western Mail*, noted:

> In forming a judgement upon the real worth of a man's life it is difficult, during his lifetime, to predict whether history will or will not keep his memory green within the knowledge of future generations ... There is, however, no doubt about the reward the future holds in its palm for the memory of Dr Griffith John, the great Welsh missionary ... The mission field has always provided heroes. It has never yet raised a man who has excelled Dr John in pioneer work and wise judgement under almost insuperable odds.

But, for all his confidence, the writer was mistaken and Griffith John's name is all but forgotten today, except in a few limited circles. Some of the reasons for this are discussed in a later chapter. What may be confidently stated, however, is that no one who has ever read the truly remarkable details of his life will easily forget him.

Representatives of two of the limited circles mentioned above were surprised when, unknowingly, they met in March 2014. A group of Chinese Christian pastors staying at Wales Evangelical School of Theology, Bridgend, visited a chapel in Swansea. All they knew was that the chapel had some connection with China. All that the minister of the church knew was that these pastors were from China. When he started talking to them of Griffith John, who was raised in, and sent out from, that chapel, he met with an excited response. The pastors inquired of their interpreter: 'Is this man speaking of *the* Griffith John?' What the minister had not known was that these pastors were from Hankou (present-day Wuhan), the centre of John's activities in China. What the pastors had not known was that the chapel was Ebenezer Chapel, where John was raised. They rejoiced that they had quite inadvertently found what they described as 'our mother-church'.

1

CHILDHOOD AND YOUTH IN SWANSEA (1831–55)

EBENEZER CHAPEL, SWANSEA

The early 1800s witnessed a rapid growth of industries in the Lower Swansea Valley. By 1820, 90% of the copper-smelting capacity of Britain was found here. The region was regarded as the world centre for copper-ore smelting and Swansea gained the nickname 'Copperopolis'. A less welcome consequence was the great influx of population, resulting in an area of overcrowded and insanitary slums in the north of the borough. Outbreaks of typhoid and scarlet fever were common. It was here that Griffith John was born on 14 December 1831, in Emma Street, Hafod. He was the fourth child of Griffith and Ann John. Six months after his birth a cholera epidemic broke out in the Hafod area of Swansea.

One hundred and fifty people died, one of them being Ann John, Griffith John's mother. His father was a foreman at the Messrs Vivian and Sons copper works. He struggled to raise the four children, all under eight years old, helped by his sister Mary. The family worshipped at Ebenezer Welsh Congregational Church, situated about 700 yards from their home in Emma Street, and the members and officers of the church also helped to raise and care for the motherless children. Ebenezer, at that time, had the largest membership of any chapel in Wales, and the early life of Griffith John was centred around it. In an autobiographical note, written as an old man, he described his early days:

> From the cradle I was brought up in a religious atmosphere. All my relations on my father's side have been known as eminent for their piety ... I have even now very vivid recollections of the prayers offered up at the Saturday evening prayer meetings by Uncles David and Rees. How they would wrestle with God! Each of them presented to my imagination a living picture of wrestling Jacob. All these godly men took the deepest interest in me. How much I owe to their prayers and loving counsel is known to God only. Then there was the Sunday School with its hallowed influences. In those days the Sunday School in Wales was a grand institution for imbuing the child's mind with Biblical knowledge and Christian principles. I seem to have been born and brought up in the House of God, and among God's people. It may be truly said of me, as it was of Timothy, 'And from a babe thou hast known the Holy Scriptures.'

Griffith John was converted at eight years of age. He had witnessed his older sister, Mary, being received into the membership of the church and the question came into his head, 'If she is right in joining the church publicly in

Childhood and youth in Swansea (1831–55)

this way, should I not consecrate my life to God, as she is doing?' His persistent self-questioning led him to speak to the deacons of the church. They encouraged him to persevere in his faith and, after some months' probation, they 'at last gave it as their united opinion that the change in the little boy was genuine, and that he ought to be admitted into Church fellowship'. This was far from being their normal practice. They must have seen very evident signs of grace in the boy.

One of the deacons, William Rees, who was also his Sunday School teacher, now took him under his wing:

> He taught me to *think*, and was the first who ever tried to do so. He put me in the way of taking down the heads of sermons, a habit which I kept up for years. Mr Rees also encouraged me to commit large portions of the Scriptures to memory. During the three years I was under his influence, I must have committed a large portion of the Psalms, as well as the Proverbs and Ecclesiastes, and the greater part of the New Testament, to memory.

Although so strange to us today, this rote learning of extensive portions of Scripture was not in any way rare in Wales at that time. Indeed, John himself commented that his cousin, who 'had a more retentive memory than I had ... went beyond me in this line of things'. William Rees also found work for him at Onllwyn, a village about twenty miles from Swansea, where he worked in the general stores of an iron and coal mining company. It was at Onllwyn that he began to preach, when only fourteen years old. He soon realised that this was a mistake and stopped, only to begin again when he was sixteen. He did not stop again for the next sixty years. His power and oratory at such a young age astounded the congregations and invitations to supply pulpits were numerous. He began to be known in south Wales as 'The Boy-Preacher'. In 1848, he returned to Swansea determined to become a preacher, and determined also to obtain a college education. The minister at Ebenezer at the time was the Rev. Elijah Jacob, who undertook to tutor him through a preparatory course of Greek and Theology:

> I commenced my studies with Mr Jacob in November 1848. All went on well till August 11, 1849, when my dear father died of cholera, the disease to which my dear mother had succumbed in 1832. My father was taken ill in the morning, and died in the evening about ten o'clock.

152 people died in Swansea during the three months of this outbreak. Elijah Jacob now stepped into the breach and became a substitute father to the seventeen-year-old boy. He continued tutoring him without payment and made all the arrangements for his entry to college. In later life John acknowledged his debt to him: 'One of the great fortunes of my life was to come into close contact with this truly noble man ... To me he was father, brother, friend.' They continued to correspond for over fifty years, through all but eight of John's years in China, until Jacob died in 1903.

CALLED TO THE MISSION FIELD

In 1850 Griffith John was accepted at the Congregational Theological College at Brecon. During his three years at the College the well-known missionary, David Griffiths of Madagascar, was living nearby. He had been forced to flee the island because of the persecution of Christians that arose when the unbelieving Queen Ranavalona came to the throne. Brecon College made use of him as a

Childhood and youth in Swansea (1831–55)

visiting lecturer. While listening to him, Griffith John was confirmed in his sense of a call to the mission field and, in particular, to the church in Madagascar.

> A large number of my ministerial friends were bitterly opposed to my taking this course. They believed in missions but they could not see that it was God's will that I should be a missionary. They spoke of my special fitness for the ministry in Wales, and pointed to the offers which I had already received from several churches as a clear indication of God's will concerning me. They loved me sincerely and were extremely anxious to save me from taking a false step. I thanked them for all their kindness, but assured them that my purpose was fixed, and that I must obey the Divine voice.

Visits to David Griffiths' home nearby at Hay-on-Wye were not only in order to derive benefit from the veteran's experience. Griffith John had fallen in love with the missionary's daughter, Margaret. She was born in Madagascar in 1830 and was twelve years old when the family had to flee the island.

In 1853 John applied to be a missionary with the London Missionary Society. In accepting him, the directors noted that it seemed that Madagascar would be a closed door to missionaries for the immediate future; their appreciation of John's abilities and strength of character led them to assign him to the much more difficult field of China. At this time he was spending some months at the LMS Missionary Academy at Bedford. As well as receiving specifically missionary-orientated training, the directors also judged that his grasp of English needed to be improved. He wrote home to Mr Jacob:

> I have complied with the request of the Directors in

respect to China. I don't know exactly when we shall be sent out, probably about the commencement of the spring. If that be the case I shall see you very soon. But there is a degree of sadness about our next meeting to which I do not like to look forward. It will be a meeting of very short duration, but followed by a parting for a very long time, probably never to see each other on earth again.

His next words demonstrate the spiritual maturity of this twenty-four year-old:

There is a glorious work before me. When looking at it, I cannot but rejoice, but with trembling. It is both humbling and cheering. Oh that I could but feel that I am not my own, and that I am thoroughly consecrated to God. How difficult it is to get rid of selfishness. The drunkard may set aside his drunkenness, the blasphemer his blasphemy, his curses and oaths, but it is almost impossible to destroy self and live, to be and not to be at the same time. Self clings to us wherever we go; we find it with us in all our engagements, however sacred they may be. This is the great demon that continually seeks the mastery over us, the old Adam that perpetually speaks within us and driving us from God and goodness. Oh, could I but feel as Paul felt when he said, 'To me to live is Christ'.

In 1855, Griffith John wrote in his diary: 'I was ordained at Ebenezer on the 6th of April. Was married on the 13th at Myddfai by Mr Jacob of Swansea.' And in a little over a month, he and Margaret set sail from Gravesend to Shanghai, China. He was 24 years old, looked even younger, and was only just over five feet tall. When he arrived with a friend at the LMS house in London for a farewell lunch before embarking, an official at the door (presumably thinking that he was too young to have been invited) grabbed him with a 'No, you don't!' His friend had to rescue him, explaining, 'Why do you detain Mr John? He is my colleague. We are going to China together.' As they continued on their way, the man was heard to say, 'So, it has come to this, sending children to convert the Chinese.'

2
SHANGHAI
(1855–61)

Until 1842, China, with its 430 million inhabitants accounting for a third of the world's population, was a completely closed country. Robert Morrison—the first Protestant missionary to China—arrived in 1807 at the Portuguese colony of Macao. In the 27 years of his missionary labours, however, he could never penetrate further into China than the trading area of Guangzhou (Canton). All that he could do was to prepare the way with the production of the first Chinese translation of the Bible. Then in 1842, as a result of the First Opium War, China was forced to open up four other ports for trading with the outside world, one of them being Shanghai.

When Griffith and Margaret John arrived in Shanghai on board the *Hamilla Mitchell* on 24 September 1855, it was only ten years or so after the very first Protestant missionaries had entered the country. In fact, they took over the London Missionary Society dwelling which had previously been rented out for some months to a young man called James Hudson Taylor. They lived, at first, among the community of LMS missionaries based at Shanghai: Walter Medhurst, the Mission's printer; Dr Lockhart, head of the Medical Mission; William Muirhead, an outstanding evangelist; Alexander Wylie and Joseph Edkins, eminent Chinese scholars. John's first task, with the help of the latter two men, was to learn the language. He noted:

> Chinese is written with curious-looking characters. They are not the symbols of sounds, like ours, but of ideas; the sounds, or names of them, change with every variation of dialect; but the ideas they represent never alter.

That is, whereas written English is *phonographic* (each letter representing a sound), the Chinese written language is *logographic*—it uses pictures or characters to represent words. This means that there are thousands of Chinese characters to be learnt. The Mandarin language that John was learning involves about 40,000 characters, of which about 6,000 are in common use. William Milne, an early missionary to China, wrote:

> To acquire the Chinese language is a work for men with bodies of brass, lungs of steel, heads of oak, hands of spring-steel, eyes of eagles, hearts of apostles, memories of angels, lives of Methuselah.

It is at this point in his life, perhaps, that the remarkable intellectual capacity of this young man, Griffith John, first strikes us. A. J. Broomhall, the pre-eminent historian of Chinese missionaries, wrote of him:

> Within a week Griffith John had memorised some simple

Shanghai (1855–61)

> Chinese phrases, enough to say, 'Do you believe in the Lord Jesus? Believing in Him is the best thing you can do ... '

Most of us, probably, when beginning to learn a language, start with such phrases as, 'Good morning', 'How are you?', 'My name is ...' Clearly, for Griffith John, other expressions were much more important.

> ... and six months later he was out in the temples and streets talking, distributing tracts and beginning to preach. After nine months he was preaching in the chapels for half an hour and more 'with considerable ease and fluency', well understood by his hearers. The average foreigner took two, three or even five years to attain the same skill. All his life evangelism was his aim and weapon. His biographer summed up his life in terms of 'amazing and tireless industry and thoroughness' and 'magnificent optimism'. The 'magnetism of his faith and enthusiasm' influenced all who came in contact with him.

This was to be the pattern of his work for the next five years. Broomhall continues:

> At Shanghai itself a phenomenon was emerging which made Hudson Taylor's daily preaching at the Southgate paltry by comparison. The born orators William Muirhead and Griffith John were developing the street chapel preaching for which they were to become famous. For five years they were at it every day, never lacking audiences.

As he was tall and fair, in contrast to the short, dark-haired Chinese, Muirhead was called a 'real devil', but the dark Welshman, not much more than five foot in height was considered a 'devil in disguise'.

Another close friend and LMS colleague was Alexander

Williamson. He and his wife had travelled out to China with Griffith and Margaret John on the *Hamilla Mitchell*. The two men learnt together the skills of preaching in Chinese as they ventured out onto the streets of Shanghai. Griffith John had great respect for his friend, although after their Shanghai days the two were to part. While John was in central China, Williamson worked in the north as a colporteur for the National Bible Society of Scotland. In those early days of an open China, he travelled more perhaps than any other missionary, taking his Bibles and New Testaments to eastern Mongolia, Beijing, Shandong, Shanxi, Shaanxi, Henan, Shantung and Manchuria.

By October 1856, Griffith John was ready for his first preaching journey out of Shanghai with only a Chinese colporteur as a companion. He had commented during an earlier journey with his colleagues that he found the Chinese 'to be the most indifferent, cold ... callous, irreligious that I have ever seen or read of', but this time he witnessed an incident that highlighted a worthier element of the Chinese character, one of which he would make much use in the years to come. A man took a book that was offered him and then tore it apart. Previously, John had seen thousands of books and tracts being accepted without ever being thrown away or ripped up by the Chinese; their Confucianism taught them to revere the written page. In this case the offender was a Roman Catholic convert! For the remainder of his life his awareness of the usefulness of the written word to reach the Chinese, and his literary efforts to take advantage of this, were such that A. J. Broomhall described him as 'the leading missionary author in Chinese'.

3

First journeys during days of rebellion

The Taiping Rebellion

Throughout the period of Griffith John's years in Shanghai a massive civil war was raging in the south of the country. The Taiping rebellion lasted from 1850 to 1864 and it is estimated that between 20 and 30 million people died as a result of it. When we recall that the total death tolls of the First and Second World Wars were estimated at 16 and 60 million respectively, the devastating effect of this rebellion is evident. Unlike the Opium Wars, which were largely a matter of pitched battles between standing armies, the Rebellion was waged as a total war between civilian populations. A scorched earth policy employed by both sides laid waste vast areas of agricultural land, the populations of defeated cities were massacred, and more than 600 cities destroyed. It was essentially a rebellion of the Han Chinese of the south against the corrupt and ineffective Manchu-led regime of the Qing Dynasty, but its complex nature typified the complexities of the politics and ethnicities of the country as a whole. A major element that confused the attitudes of the Western powers towards the civil war was that the leader of the Taiping, Hong Xiuquan, claimed that he had received visions from God and that he was the younger brother of Jesus Christ. The reforms for which he fought included the replacement of the traditional Chinese religions by his own form of Christianity. Many of the missionaries in the land argued that the rebels should be supported. All recognised the need for political and educational reform in China and, for a period early on in the rebellion, before the more fanatical delusions of Hong were realised, it was thought that the work of the gospel would be considerably more prosperous under a Taiping government than under the Imperial regime. Griffith John, with his optimistic nature, was initially considerably encouraged by the successes of the Taiping Heavenly Kingdom armies.

'Epic journeys'

The ravages of the civil war were not to arrive at the neighbourhood of Shanghai until the late 1850s, and during the period from 1857 to 1859 Griffith John was able to make longer and longer journeys into the hinterland beyond the port. In 1857 he wrote, 'The people of Shanghai take no more interest in the Canton war than they do in the Indian ... The people here are as well disposed as ever.' In the interior also they had preached to many thousands, and had met with no opposition or difficulties arising from the rebellion. This being the case John, together with Joseph Edkins, made a pioneering journey to the city of Suzhou, some 70 miles to the west of Shanghai. They were the first foreigners ever to visit this city without being in disguise. Then, in April 1858, he journeyed to the previously unfriendly city of Hangzhou in the south-west, 140 miles away, and managed to distribute 6,000 New Testaments. By this time, Lockhart, Williamson and Edkins (all LMS colleagues) had, for various reasons, returned temporarily to Britain, but such was John's growing confidence that he, his wife, and their three-year old boy, also Griffith, had moved from Shanghai and had settled on their own in Pinghu, about 80 miles south of the international port. From here, he established out-stations in the surrounding cities of Suzhou, Wuxing, Songjiang and Hangzhou. A. J. Broomhall's description of him at this time notes that, 'Griffith John was always on the move. His Welsh exuberance could not be content with routine duties in the city of Shanghai. But he himself admitted thirty years later that in those early days, he "knew more about how things should be done than all his seniors". Their lack of success, he held, was due to lack of insight. So he was appointed to country itineration to absorb his energy.'

In June 1859, Griffith John and Andrew Muirhead travelled further than any of their Shanghai colleagues had done. The city of Suzhou, only reached two years previously, now became the springboard to launch them on their way to Changzhou, where they crossed the Yangzi and proceeded on the old bed of the Yellow River to Qingjiang, three hundred miles from Shanghai. This was the furthest yet that Protestant missionaries had penetrated China. Tensions were increasing, however, between the Chinese and the Western governments. A refusal by the dynasty to ratify the Tientsin Treaty of 1858 led to a clash of armies. Anti-foreign feelings began to spread. Muirhead and John found that they had returned from the west only just in time. Missionaries and converts met with persecution and attacks, which were spurred on by encouragement from Beijing.

But worse was to follow. In the spring of 1860, the Taiping gained significant victories over the Imperial army and, travelling eastward from their base at Nanjing, they sacked the beautiful cities of Suzhou and Hanzhou. All the preaching stations that John had established in the previous three years were swept away. The main rebel objective now was to take Shanghai.

INTO REBEL TERRITORY

There was still no consensus among the missionaries in their attitude towards the rebels, although the majority were beginning to doubt the reality of any true Christian influence upon Hong Xiuquan and his aides. Griffith John remained optimistic and was determined to find out for himself. In July 1860, he, Joseph Edkins and two other colleagues set out for Suzhou, the local headquarters of the 'Taiping Heavenly Kingdom'.

This was, perhaps, his most dangerous journey yet. 'Passing through no-man's-land between free and rebel territory brought them under fire from both sides. On the fourth night their canal boat had to push through log jams of decomposing corpses, suicides and victims of Taiping savagery. Rather than fall into rebel hands, men, women and children of the upper, moneyed classes took their own lives. When the party joined a body of a hundred horse and foot, they found them friendly ... Finally they reached the rebel leaders at Suzhou, secure among thirty thousand insurgents—and were favourably impressed.' They were

First journeys during days of rebellion

granted several interviews with Hong Xiuquan, saw the use made of Old and New Testaments in the worship of the Taiping, and presented gifts of Bibles and books. On departing after a two-week visit, they were invited to return again.

After a second visit in August, A. J. Broomhall notes, 'Edkins and Griffith John were still impressed, but to John Burdon the gross errors in the Taiping creed excluded co-operation and hope of reform.'

The Taiping attack upon Shanghai effectively ended the neutral stance of the British and the French towards the civil war. They made their peace with Beijing, and European officers were provided to train and lead the Chinese soldiers. The resulting new army, led by the Englishman Charles Gordon (known to us today as Gordon of Khartoum but to his fellow-Victorians as "Chinese" Gordon), was instrumental in defeating the rebel forces. By 1864 the Emperor was again in control of most of the country.

Long before this time, the increasingly delusional and blasphemous nature of Hong Xiuquan's beliefs had become apparent, and even Griffith John had had to acknowledge that, 'the spurious Christianity which they pretend to profess was utterly unworthy of any Christian sympathy.' It may be that in maintaining a positive view of the rebel leaders for so long, months after others had given up on them, Griffith John's natural optimism had for once let him down, and his senior colleagues with their years of experience of Chinese politics had been the wiser heads.

By now, the John family had two children. Griffith, the older boy, had been born in 1855, and David in 1859. In

1860, little Griffith, now five years old, was sent home to Wales under the care of Alexander Wylie, who was returning to Britain. Griffith John wrote to Elijah Jacob:

> You seem all of you to be greatly surprised at our sending him so young. We are astonished at ourselves, and I doubt whether we shall ever be equal to another such trial. I am still convinced it was the best course that we could take in the circumstances. It is impossible to bring up children, especially boys, as they should be brought up in China. Some of the most ungodly young men in China are missionaries' children ... In *Mei foh*'s [Griffith's Chinese name] case we find that every summer tells more and more on his constitution. The last brought him very low.

David, their second son was sent home similarly in 1864. Faithful, godly Elijah Jacob acted as father to the two boys back in Swansea, as he had done to their father before them.

4

The Opium Wars

The 1842 Treaty of Nanking stated that foreigners were only allowed to travel a distance that was less than a day's journey from any of the four open ports. Griffith John's interpretation of the treaty was such that in these five years he had visited and preached at all the towns within a radius of about one hundred and fifty miles around Shanghai. The progress of the work fluctuated because of the ongoing Second Opium War. Thus in 1858 he had preached openly in Hangzhou, distributed literature and established a preaching station there; but by 1860 the city was closed to all foreign people. The LMS work in the region around Shanghai was well established by that date. Griffith John was now experienced in the work and was becoming increasingly aware of areas and peoples, hundreds of miles to the west, never before visited by Protestant missionaries. Europeans were still forbidden to travel inland, but this situation was soon to alter.

THE OPENING UP OF CHINA

In 1860, by the mysterious ways of God's providence, international political events were to change Griffith John's life completely. The Bible teaches that the ambitions and evils of ungodly men are used by God in his purposes for his church. He used the cruelty and greed of an Assyrian army to afflict and chastise Israel; he made use of Roman conquests to open up opportunities of travel for Paul and for the gospel. There is no more remarkable example than the opening up of China to Christian missionaries.

To appreciate this, the history of the Opium Wars must be understood. In the mid-eighteenth century, the Chinese authorities restricted access to foreign merchants to one port only—that of Canton (Guangzhou). The demand for Chinese goods—tea, silk, porcelain—in Victorian Britain was huge. But all of this had to be paid for in cash. There was no market in China for anything that Britain manufactured. The balance of payments between the two countries became uncomfortably large. Desperate to find a new market in China, Britain began importing opium into China. The Indian opium fields were completely under the control of the British East India Company. The addictive nature of opium soon established the market! The trade in opium from the Bengali fields into Canton grew from 15 tons annually in 1730 to 75 tons in 1773 and 1,400 tons by 1838.

Responding to the fact that a significant proportion of the population had become addicted, the Chinese government banned the importation, and prohibited the use, of opium; but they could not prevent the trade continuing by smuggling. Their attempted blockade of

British trading ships led to the First Opium War (1839–1842) between Britain and China. British warships and troops from India took Canton, and forced the Chinese government to sue for peace. The resulting Treaty of Nanking in 1842 required China to open up four more ports (including Shanghai) for trade. In the next decade relationships worsened and the Second Opium War (1856–60) broke out when China sought again to combat the increasing opium smuggling. Its result was inevitable: a British/French army of 18,000 defeated a Chinese army of 30,000 in 1860 and forced the Chinese to agree to the terms of the Treaty of Tientsin (Tianjin). The major points of the treaty were:

1. Britain, France, Russia, and the USA would have the right to establish diplomatic legations (small embassies) in Peking (Beijing)—a closed city at the time.

2. Ten more Chinese ports would be opened for foreign trade, including Niuzhuang, Tamsui, Hankou, and Nanjing.

3. The right of all foreign vessels, including commercial ships, to navigate freely on the Yangzi River.

4. The right of foreigners to travel in the internal regions of China, which had formerly been banned.

5. China was to pay an indemnity to Britain and France of 8 million taels of silver each.

The second and fourth of these points were the more significant ones as far as Griffith John was concerned.

In this way, China was opened to the gospel by the greedy, selfish and hypocritical bullying of an imperialistic nation. 'Surely the wrath of men shall praise Thee', says the Psalmist. But God's over-ruling providence does not mean that evil actions can be justified. The flooding of China with opium purely for economic gain went on for another thirty years. In China, the actions of the British government were taken as a standard of Christian morality and greatly hindered missionary work. Griffith John consistently deplored the vicious trade. He wrote in 1856:

> I saw today for the first time opium smoking. This is the very bane of China. To see men under the influence of this cursed stuff is sickening and heart-rending.

And thirty years later his attitude was the same:

> The trade has damaged the Christian name in China to an extent hardly conceived by people at home. Not only has it retarded the progress of Christianity by creating a strong prejudice against us, the preachers of it; it has brought Christianity itself into contempt.

In 1890, Griffith John helped to establish the Permanent Committee for the Promotion of Anti-Opium Societies, comprised of British and American missionaries, with the aim of arousing public awareness of the evils of the trade. Eventually, the importing of opium by Britain, through its Indian trade routes, was more or less stopped by 1910. Opium smoking was not finally eradicated in the country until after the Chinese Communists came into power in 1949.

5
Hankou (1861–70)
–First Steps

Hankou, in the province of Hubei, stands at the confluence of the rivers Yangzi and Han. Along the banks of the rivers, three walled cities faced each other—Hankou, Wuchang and Hanyang (together they constitute the present-day Wuhan). Hankou had, at that time, a population of over two million, and the other two cities each had over a million inhabitants. Their position lay at the very heart of Central China. The Yangzi River, over 600 miles west of its entry into the sea at Shanghai, was still a mile wide at this point, and extended westward for another 3,400 miles. The Han River had its source nearly 1,000 miles to the north-west. Between them, the two rivers ensured that Hankou was the centre of culture, finance, trade and transport for the whole of Central China. Its mart was the largest in the country. Wuchang served as the administrative centre of both Hubei province and Hunan province, two of the eighteen provinces of China. Their total population in 1860 was about sixty million, a greater number than the population of the British Isles at the time. There were no Protestant missionaries or Protestant churches anywhere in the province.

Arrival at Hankou

For years Griffith John had had his eye on Hankou. Once the Treaty of Tientsin had been ratified, he undertook the dangerous journey up the Yangzi with Robert Wilson, another LMS missionary, arriving at the city on 21 June 1861 after sailing for twelve days. He noted in his journal:

> It would be impossible for me to describe my feelings when I found myself actually at Hankou. I could hardly believe that I was standing in the very centre of that China that had been closed till then against the outer barbarian, and that it would be my privilege on the very next day to appear as a missionary of the Cross in the streets of the famous city. I thought of the great and good men who had been longing to see what I was seeing, but did not see it. I thought of Milne, who, on his arrival at Canton, knocked earnestly for admittance, but was ruthlessly driven away. I thought of Morrison, who knocked for twenty-six years, but died without having received the promise. I thought of Medhurst, and remembered the last prayer I heard him offer up at Shanghai: 'O God, open China, and scatter Thy servants.' I thought of these and many others, who had laboured long and well in the days gone by, and felt as if they were present on this occasion, beholding my joy and rejoicing with me in the triumph of Divine providence over China's exclusiveness. I felt that I had got at last to the place where God would have me be, and my heart was at rest.

Hankou (1861–70)—first steps

He stayed long enough to rent 'a small native house in a narrow lane in one of the most densely populated quarters of the Chinese city ... [in] dark and evil-smelling surroundings'. He returned to Shanghai to collect Margaret and the two young children, and was back in Hankou in September.

His first work typified what was to be the set pattern of work for over fifty years—preaching the gospel and distributing literature:

> As we have no regular chapel, the services are conducted in a large hall in my house. The door is open every afternoon for two or three hours. The native assistants (two in number) [these had joined them from Shanghai some four months later] and myself preach in turns. At the close of the service books are given away to all applicants who can read ... The Gospel is listened to invariably with much attention. Most come with the sole purpose of learning what this new doctrine is.

THE FIRST CHURCH IN CENTRAL CHINA

But as far as spiritual fruit was concerned, the first few months were discouraging: 'The people are dead in their sins. They listen, they ask a few questions, they express their satisfaction, they compliment you and your doctrine, and they leave as little moved as the benches on which they are sitting.' Then, on Sunday 16 March 1862, the first Protestant convert in Central China was baptized, on confession of his faith. Within three months, six others, four men and two women, were also baptized. By the end of 1862, the first Protestant church in inland China had been constituted. Its membership was seventeen: Mr and Mrs John, Mr and Mrs Robert Wilson, two Shanghai believers and eleven Hankou converts. Griffith John wrote a small hymn-book in the Easy Wen-Li language for the church's use. The first chapel was built in 1863. Situated in the heart of the city and on one of its main streets, its very location soon increased the interest shown in it and the numbers in the congregation.

It is worth noting that Griffith John arrived at Hankou eight years before Hudson Taylor ventured into the interior. Taylor, who founded the China Inland Mission in 1865, did not set up a CIM station inland until about 1869.

However, the sacrifices demanded by pioneering missionary work were always present. In 1861, Griffith and Margaret's third child, a baby boy, died; the following year the same thing happened to their fourth child, another baby boy. Then, in 1863, their fellow-missionary Robert Wilson died. Hankou was known then, as now, as 'the Furnace of China'; the temperature in the summer would reach 100°F in the shade for weeks on end. All three deaths were from dysentery due to the insanitary conditions and the extreme heat. Their first daughter, Mary, was born in 1863. By 1864 the church membership had risen to 23; and they as a family moved to a new home in healthier surroundings.

The first permanent extension of the work was the setting up of a mission station at nearby Wuchang. For many months Griffith John had to endure patiently the wrath of Mandarins, scholars and gentry as they fought to refuse him permission to buy property in the city. Eventually, a Wuchang convert, Pau Ting Chang was stationed there as a native evangelist; and when Thomas Bryson arrived from England in 1867 he was placed there and directed the Wuchang LMS station for the next seventeen years. In the same year a preaching station was set up in the third city, Hangyang. The cost of building the Wuchang centre was donated to the LMS by members of the increasing European community at Hankou. The centre at Hangyang was both funded and manned by members of the Hankou church, whose membership had risen to 108 by 1867.

ITINERATION IN HUBEI

In 1866, another LMS colleague, Evan Bryant, from Hirwaun, south Wales, had joined Griffith John at Hankou and was to remain with him until 1880. With both Bryant and Bryson able to take on major responsibilities, Griffith John could now extend his preaching itineraries throughout the Hubei province, encouraging groups of believers and establishing preaching stations. He was helped in this by a further gift from his European friends at Hankou of a river boat, which he would use for two-to-three-week trips along the Han and Yangzi rivers. His description of a later journey made in 1876 to the Hiau-kan (Xiaogan) region of Hubei, about thirty-five miles northwest of Hankou, shows that he could never be certain what kind of welcome he might receive:

> On 31st January, Dr Mackenzie and myself left Hankou with the view of visiting the converts in those parts, and doing all in our power on the way by means of teaching and healing. Everything went well with us until we came within a mile or two of the Wei village. That part of the country having never been visited by a foreigner before, we had to encounter along the whole journey the usual excitement connected with the missionary's first visit to a place, and for this we were quite prepared. But the villagers, so far from

attempting to injure us, seemed glad to see us ... When, however we came to a group of villages distant from the Wei village about two miles, the whole aspect of things changed, and we soon found ourselves exposed to an attack, the violence of which surpassed anything I have ever witnessed in China ...

It became evident at once that the people of these villages had combined to assault us in order to make it impossible for foreigners to visit their part of the country again. I tried to remonstrate with them in a way that I have often done in similar circumstances with perfect success: but it was worse than useless in this case. Remonstrance only intensified their rage. They commenced with hooting and yelling; but they soon proceeded to pelt us with lumps of hard clay. Fortunately for us there were no stones lying about. Dr Mackenzie, though not wounded, was struck scores of times. I received two cuts, one on the face and one on the head. The general cries were, "Beat the foreigners—Kill the foreigners—Back with them to Hankou—Let them go and preach in Hankou—We won't have them come here and preach." One man had a large club in his hand; another had a rapier; and many looked like very fiends.

About a mile on this side of the Wei village there is a creek which had to be crossed ere we could reach our destination. When we came to this spot there must have been a thousand people at least gathered on the banks. The villagers on one side wanted to drive us over the creek, and those on the other side threatened to kill us if we came within their reach. We ventured to attempt it; but the moment I set my foot on the bridge, I was saluted with a perfect shower of hard lumps of mud. We made our way back from this dangerous position

Hankou (1861–70)—first steps

as soon as possible; and though an attempt was made to force us on, we succeeded in regaining the bank.

From what I have heard since as well as what I saw at the time, I feel convinced that if we had not retreated we should have been murdered. Seeing that to proceed was simply impossible, I asked permission of the mob to return to Hankou, and, to my astonishment, obtained it …

The conduct of the converts and many of their friends exceeded my most sanguine expectations. When they were informed of our difficulties, they hastened to our rescue, identified themselves with us, and did all in their power to protect us. One of our friends insisted on walking side by side with me in order to shield me from harm. This noble act exposed him to many a hard blow; but he bore it all bravely and cheerfully. Another of our converts in the very height of the storm begged the mob to kill him, but spare the pastor.

Griffith John's response to this violence was one that he made use of on more than one occasion. He laid a statement before the British consul complaining of an attack on British subjects travelling within their treaty rights. The consul then passed on the complaint to the Chinese authorities and the local magistrates were warned. Within a few months Griffith John had returned to the area and the acceptance of his preaching and the subsequent spread of the gospel was remarkable. The chapel building in the Wei village was the first in Central China to be built and funded entirely by Chinese converts. By 1905 there were 2,400 members in the churches of the Hiau-Kan (Xiaogan) region.

A NIGHT ON THE ROAD

A description of a lodging place on another of his later travels is typical of his itinerating experiences throughout his years in China:

> We had no difficulty in finding an inn ... But, oh, what wretched holes these inns are! In these parts they are specially dark, dingy and in every way filthy. The floor and walls are mud, and the tiled ceiling is black with the soot of ages ... The lodger has the choice between a 'lofty bed' and a 'floor bed'. The 'lofty bed' consists of a low wooden framework covered with a thick layer of straw. The 'floor bed' consists of a straw mattress laid on the bare mud floor. The foreigner who wishes to sleep in peace must avoid both beds; for the pulex (aye, and companions more objectionable than pulex) abounds in these inns. The native beds are places where the aphaniptera, the anoplura, the heteroptera, and all kinds of unclean animals delight to hold their nocturnal revelries ...
>
> My plan in travelling overland is to secure two benches and a door, or two square tables, at every inn, and have my own bedding laid upon the top. In this way I manage to get beyond the leaps and bites of these little tormentors. In these inns the lodger is almost sure to have two or more pigs for chums. Just as we were going to ascend our lofty beds the pigs were brought in, and one by one they made their beds in front of our bedroom door. After a little squealing and grunting on their part, we all settled down for the night, and both they and ourselves were soon drowned in deep slumber.

6

'A PERILOUS JOURNEY' (1866) AND A VISIT HOME (1870)

However, Griffith John was not content with these local visits within a hundred miles or so of Hankou. His plans were considerably more ambitious. He first wrote of them in a letter to his directors in 1868:

> Were it not for the state of the finances, I would like to ask your permission to go and try and establish a mission in Chengdu, the capital of Sichuan. What say you to my bearing this in mind? Long has it been a cherished prospect of mine.

SAILING UP THE YANGZI

In April 1868, together with his friend from Shanghai days, Alexander Wylie of the British and Foreign Bible Society, two colporteurs and two servants, he began the journey. They had with them twenty-six boxes of Scriptures to distribute in the various cities along the way. Their destination, Chengdu, was over a thousand miles away.

From there they would travel overland in a north-westerly direction to reach the source of the Han River and then sail back down to Hankou.

The Yangzi is about 4,000 miles long; the longest river in Asia; the third longest in the world. Its river basin is home to a third of China's population. The missionaries were familiar with the 700-mile stretch eastward from Hankou down to the East China Sea at Shanghai. They were now to travel westward upon it for over 700 miles. Very few Europeans, except for Roman Catholic missionaries, usually in disguise, had penetrated this far beyond Hankou. Passing through the cities of Shishou, Shashi and Yichang, selling and distributing Scriptures at each stop, they arrived at the region of the Three Gorges. Today, this is one of the foremost tourist attractions of China—a hundred miles of spectacular mountains, cliffs and gorges with the great river flowing through. In 1906, Wardlaw Thompson described it as being 'of such exceptional grandeur that words altogether fail to convey any adequate sense of its majestic size and wonderful variety of form and colouring'. Griffith John's own description was:

> Nature in these regions presents a grand spectacle. Every day do we pass through some of the noblest works of God. One's thoughts are powerfully directed to the Infinite and Eternal in beholding these sublime scenes.

Today also, due to the building of the Three Gorges Dam in 2003—a scheme involving the largest comprehensive irrigation scheme in the world together with the world's largest hydro-electric scheme—the river is navigable; but in 1868 it presented considerable dangers. To ascend the rapids anything up to fifty men were employed along the

'A perilous journey' (1866) and a visit home (1870)

towpath, pulling their boat against the current. At one of the narrowest parts of the river two hundred men on bamboo lines four or five hundred yards long were needed to pull the vessel through. They saw more than one of the boats that sailed alongside them being wrecked or sunk during the passage of the Three Gorges.

Soon after passing through Chongqing, where they stayed for five days, they left the Yangzi and proceeded on one of its many tributaries, the Min, for the last 300 miles to Chendu, the political centre of Sichuan. Another 300 miles westward as the crow flies would have brought them to the China/Tibet border, and they would have traversed the whole of the country as it was then constituted. (Tibet became part of the People's Republic of China after its invasion in 1951.) When, later, Griffith John had returned to Hankou, he wrote in confidence to Elijah Jacob with words, according to Wardlaw Thompson, 'which afford a glimpse of his inner thoughts, while there is a tone in them which tells of overstrain':

> Telling you the truth, my dear brother, I hardly expected to come back. My brightest hope was that God would permit me to see Chendu, where, I thought, I could die in peace, knowing that my grave at that great and distant city would stimulate others to come and occupy it in the name of the Lord. Here I felt a thrill of the true missionary spirit which I value more than many years of ordinary life ... There are two ways of looking at the work: the one is the prudential one which you refer to, and the other is the enterprising, doing, soul-stirring one, of which the great Apostle to the Gentiles is our greatest type and representative. Most former missionaries are satisfied with the former. I long for the latter.

From Chendu they struck out overland in a north-easterly direction, crossing into the Shaanxi province and arriving at the Han River near its source at Hanzhong. From here the river took them nearly a thousand miles back home to Wuhan. The whole journey had taken five months and they had distributed and sold 71 Old Testaments, 935 New Testaments and 9059 portions of Scripture. It had proved 'one of the longest, and, in some respects, the most interesting missionary journey that has ever been made in China in modern times ... almost if not quite unprecedented in the history of Europeans.'

A visit home and Margaret's death

In 1864, Margaret John had had to return to Britain. She had been through five pregnancies in the nine years she had been in China, and been bereaved of two of the babies. Furthermore, the climate and conditions in Hankou had so undermined her own health that a period of recovery was essential. She took with her their second boy, to be left at Swansea with Elijah Jacob, and with Griffith, their eldest child. Margaret spent a year at home and returned in better health in 1865. In the following year, Griffith John built a small hospital in Hankou and she served there as a nurse and as its first matron. Two more children were born to her, a son in 1867 and a daughter in 1870, both of whom died as infants. Only three children, therefore, of the seven born to them were to survive into childhood. Margaret's health was now precarious again and further relief from the work and climate was essential for her. Griffith John, though he did not believe in furloughs, was feeling the strain of fifteen years without stop, and he accompanied her. They landed in England on 30 September 1870.

'A perilous journey' (1866) and a visit home (1870)

In London their first priority was to meet their two boys, now aged fifteen and eleven. This proved 'a bitter-sweet experience' in that the two boys did not recognize their parents. The eldest boy had not seen his father for ten years! There were changes back in Swansea also. A new, larger, Ebenezer Chapel had been built in 1862 on the same site as the original. It was considerably larger than the chapel from which Griffith John had departed and now completely covered the small graveyard that once adjoined the old chapel. This meant that he could not now visit his parents' grave. Deputation work in Wales for the LMS quickly filled his time. He found that it cost him 'a desperate effort to get the old language back'; but once he had done so the calls upon him increased still further as the Welsh churches realised he was available to preach. More and more of his Welsh friends argued with him that his duty was to stay in Wales. But his own mind was fixed and, more importantly, so was Margaret's:

> It would be impossible for me to return were it not for the genuineness of Mrs John's missionary character. She will leave without any expectation of seeing her children again, and she is hardly fit to leave the house at all; still it is her settled conviction that it is my *duty* to return, and it is her fixed resolve to accompany me.

They set sail in February 1873, but Margaret's condition worsened and she died during the voyage, long before they got to China. She was a brave and godly Welshwoman, born in Madagascar, who laboured faithfully in China for eighteen years and whose body lies in Singapore—it might well be that no one now knows where she is buried.

7

Hankou—

THE YEARS OF SERVICE

As a Christian missionary, Griffith John attempted to serve the Chinese people according to the pattern provided by his great exemplar—Jesus Christ. The Christian teaching that he wished to convey to them was of Jesus Christ as a Saviour both of the body and of the soul. He therefore had to provide for both body and soul—to serve their material needs as well as their spiritual needs. We find that the various aspects of his ministry, as it developed in Hankou from 1861 onwards, were typical of the ministries of Christian missionaries throughout the centuries. This chapter spans the years from 1861 to his retirement in 1911 and considers the educational and medical aspects of his work. These were important, but they were not his priorities, as chapter 8 will show.

Educational developments

Within six months of establishing a church at Hankou, a

boys' school was begun. In 1874, when five boys' schools were operating, John began the daring innovation of establishing a girls' school—daring, in that education was not provided for girls in China at that time. The curriculum in all the schools had to acknowledge Chinese priorities—the classic writings of China had to be taught, for example—but Bible teaching was not in any way neglected. All the teaching was in Chinese. Not until much later, around 1897, when the schools had long since been accepted and Western education was being sought, was English placed on the curriculum.

By 1897, the mission's education programme providing for the growing wants of the Christian community amounted to numerous primary schools for boys and girls, a girls' boarding school, a secondary school, and a teacher-training school. All had been established long before the Chinese state began to legislate for general education. In 1901 Griffith John wrote:

> Three remarkable Imperial decrees on education have recently been issued ... The first of these decrees was that abolishing in all public examinations the 'Wen Chang' or Chinese essay, and substituting for it essays ... on modern subjects ... [The second requires] all colleges to be turned into schools of Western learning. Every county is to have a primary school, every prefecture is to have a second grade school, and every provincial capital is to have a college.

Areas within the provinces of Hubei and Hunan were therefore years ahead of other provinces in this respect (thirty years ahead, in the case of Hankou). Towards the end of the nineteenth century Christian missionaries were being consulted by the government for guidance and help

MEDICAL DEVELOPMENTS

Griffith John built his first hospital in Hankou in 1866. It could accommodate up to twenty patients. A sum of £300 was collected for the work. The largest donation came from other foreigners living in the city; the next largest sum was from the Chinese natives themselves; the third was from the governor of the province. A second hospital, replacing the first, was built in 1874 at a cost of £1,350. Then, in 1891, a hospital for women was opened. This was financed primarily by Griffith John himself as a memorial to his first wife. He named it *The Margaret John Memorial Hospital* and it helped to break down even further the Chinese objection to the use of women missionaries at Hankou. The Chinese women were happier being treated by female doctors, and this paved the way for other female Christian workers.

By 1901, the LMS Mission was in charge of a large, well-equipped general hospital and a women's hospital in Hankou, and five other general hospitals, a women's hospital, and a leper asylum, elsewhere in the two provinces of Hubei and Hunan. These provided a total of 350 beds for in-patients. Much of the work in these hospitals was taken up with the treatment of opium addicts. A Medical School had also been established in Hankou to train Chinese Christians to become medical evangelists.

Griffith John would raise the money to build these schools and hospitals by appealing to his friends—missionary colleagues, Europeans from the professional and commercial communities in Hankou, and the growing number of Chinese converts. Because, in his early years at Hankou, he had refused to receive a salary for his ministry to the European community, they responded by contributing generously. By the time a permanent English chaplain was appointed, after John had been preaching to them for four years, he calculated that they had given over £2,500 to his various appeals. In later years he would contribute large sums himself. In this way, he was able to act quickly without having to wait for financial support from the LMS and from home churches.

Theological training

Wardlaw Thompson noted that 'As the number of converts increases, as the Bible gets into the hands of the people, and the Church is organised, and questions are asked, and difficulties arise, it becomes absolutely necessary that the leaders of the Church should be trained men.' The first systematic effort to meet this need at Hankou was the establishing in 1891 of a conference for Chinese evangelists and deacons. Lectures were delivered on 'Pastoral Theology', 'Prophecy', 'Biblical Exegesis' and 'The Epistle to the Hebrews'. Sessions for discussing practical matters were also included, on which Griffith John commented:

> The three sittings for the discussion of native customs were full of deep interest to us all. Among the subjects discussed by us the following stood out prominently: the practice of usury, opium-smoking, gambling, theatre-going, foot-binding, early betrothals, ancestral worship, funeral and wedding rites and customs. We wanted ... to find out the views entertained by our native helpers as to the attitude which the converts should assume in regard to them. They

were encouraged to speak out their minds fully and freely, and not allow themselves to be influenced in the least by the presence of the missionaries or the opinions supposed to be held by them ... We were soon made to feel that we were dealing with men who had thought for themselves on all practical subjects connected with Christian work, and who had arrived at clear views, and possessed deep convictions on every point.

It is our intention to hold these conferences twice a year ... but even this will not meet their needs and the requirements of their work. The time is coming, and it is not too far distant, when the Hankou Mission will be compelled to take into serious consideration a scheme for thorough training of native agents.

Thirteen years later, in 1904, the Hankou Theological College was opened. Griffith John had paid for this himself and presented it as a gift to the LMS. It was 'a handsome two-storey red-brick building, with verandah on four sides. It contains a lecture hall capable of seating two hundred, library and class-rooms and dormitories, with accommodation for sixty students.'

8
Griffith John's priorities

Although educational and medical help was important, Griffith John's main purpose in China was to bring the gospel to the Chinese people. To this end, he constantly emphasised three priorities. In 1882 he listed them as follows: 'In order to obtain the best possible results, you require three things—the Scriptures, the tract, and the living voice.'

'The Scriptures'

When Griffith John arrived in China, two versions of the Scriptures were in use. The first, the 'Delegates' Version', was the work of scholars from among the Shanghai missionaries. Beginning in 1847, they had completed the Bible by 1853, and it was the version adopted by the British and Foreign Bible Society. It was written in the highest possible classical style. Known as High Wen-Li, it was the classical language of the scholar. Men of general education used a plainer, more modern form described as Easy Wen-Li. The second version, a translation of the New Testament only and completed in 1867, was the work of missionaries in the north of the country. This was written in colloquial Mandarin, a language used in the whole of North China down to the Yangzi River, and used by more than half the population of China. This version, however, was open to objection as a Bible translation because of its lack of literary style.

In 1883, Griffith John began to translate the Gospels into Easy Wen-Li. He progressed so successfully that by 1885 he had completed the first translation of the New Testament into the Wen-Li language. Very early in the work of translating, when he had completed a version of Mark's Gospel in Easy Wen-Li, the National Bible Society of Scotland gave him a grant of £5 to produce a thousand copies so that these might be distributed among colleagues and its acceptability judged.

The expressions received were so favourable, and were accompanied with so many orders for the book, that more printing and further translations followed as a matter of course ... In fact, so general was the acceptance of the work, that the following letter was addressed to Mr John on 20 December 20 1887:

> The Committees of the British and Foreign Bible Society and the National Bible Society of Scotland have unanimously and very cordially agreed to join in a request which it is now our privilege to submit to you, namely, that you should undertake the preparation of a new Mandarin Colloquial Version for China, to be published on the joint responsibility and at the joint cost of the two Societies ... We are deeply impressed with the importance and necessity of this work, to

Griffith John's priorities

which, assured of your pre-eminent qualifications for it, we venture to call you.

Griffith John did not take up this offer because of certain conditions laid down by the Societies with which he did not agree; but he revised his Easy Wen-Li version of the New Testament and then produced a colloquial Mandarin version in a style that he hoped would meet with more general acceptance than the 1867 version. By 1890, many thousands of pounds had been spent by the Bible Society of Scotland, and more than six million copies of various Scriptures in John's translations into the two languages had been distributed. The New Testament, the Psalms and Proverbs were available in both languages. Later he took up the work again; and by the time of his final illness he had completed the Old Testament in Easy Wen-Li and translated up to the Book of Isaiah in Mandarin.

In these few paragraphs are described twenty-five years of work: work which Griffith John undertook in his spare moments, when his other duties of organising, itinerating and preaching allowed him. It was for this work, however, that he was honoured when the University of Edinburgh conferred upon him the honorary title of Doctor of Divinity in 1889. His only reference to the matter is found in a letter to Elijah Jacob where he says that he does not feel at home or at all comfortable in the new honour.

'THE TRACT'

The Chinese had a great respect, even a reverence, for anything in print. Realising this, Griffith John began writing Chinese tracts from the moment he arrived in the country. But after his return from his first visit to Britain in

1873 he gave more of his time to literary work. A timetable of a week-day during this period would read:

> 8.30 am to 1.00 pm: Study; 'writing books, tracts, or letters ... reading and expounding important native or foreign works'.
>
> 1.00 pm to 2.00 pm: Lunch.
>
> 2.30 pm to 5.00 pm: Chapel; 'preaching, talking, debating'.
>
> 6.00 pm onwards: Vestry; receiving any who may wish to converse on Christian subjects.

In 1875 he formed the *Hankou Tract Society*, funded by a £50 gift received from the British *Religious Tract Society*. Its purpose to begin with was to help finance the purchase and distribution of the few available tracts; but this small supply produced a great demand, and the president of the society was soon hard-pressed to write and print sufficient material to meet the demand. Not that he 'wrote' the tracts himself:

> The ability to *write* the [Chinese characters] is by no means essential to thorough efficiency in speaking and reading, whilst these two are the only branches which a foreigner can ever hope to master. Chinese *composition* appears to be beyond our reach. I have never seen a production by a foreigner which in a literary point of view did not excite the ridicule of an ordinary native scholar. The consequence is that most of the missionaries leave the writing to the Chinese pundits, whilst they exert their energies on the more feasible and vastly more important accomplishments of reading and speaking with ease, accuracy and fullness. When they want to publish, they convey to the pundit the substance *viva voce*, which he puts into good idiomatic Chinese. Though the

missionary may not be able to compose himself, he ought to be able to form a critical judgement of the composition of his pundit. This power is acquired in course of time in connection with extensive reading, and it is all that is necessary in order to turn out productions of incomparably greater value than the missionary can ever hope to turn out by his own unaided ability.

After eight years' work the name of the society was changed to *The Central China Religious Tract Society*. Its growth in production was remarkable. In 1876 it had produced 9,000 tracts and booklets. In 1883 this had become 340,000, and 2.2 million in 1903. A colportage branch was set up to speed the distribution, and by 1903 this employed seventy colporteurs in the provinces of Hubei and Henan. The tracts were used throughout China, and also in Korea and Japan. In later years, orders were received at Hankou from Jamaica, the USA, Australia, and in fact from every part of the world where Chinese people were to be found in any numbers.

Griffith John had been the president of this society from the outset and edited all that it published. Indeed, he was the author of much of the literature distributed. Of the fifty titles published in 1884, thirty-one were by him. These included a wide range: apologetic titles like *The Gate of Virtue and Wisdom*, aimed at the typical Chinese classic scholar; evangelistic tracts like *The Need of Repentance, The Forgiveness of Sins*; theological essays such as *On Regeneration, The Atonement, The Doctrine of Resurrection, The True Saviour of the World*; textbooks like *A Catechism of Christian Doctrine, Great Themes of the Gospel*; moral teachings—for example, *A Cure for the Opium Habit, The Parent*.

Hudson Taylor told the Committee of the National Bible Society of Scotland in 1884 that Mr John was, 'the author of most of the Hankou series of tracts, which in the judgement of many of us were far and away the best prepared and best adapted Christian tracts we ever had in China'. D. E. Hoste, Hudson Taylor's successor, wrote, in 1905, 'It is no exaggeration to say that this particular branch of Dr John's work has provided China with a clear, concise statement of sound, evangelical doctrine, the value of which cannot be over-estimated.'

'THE LIVING VOICE'

But, above all else, the one activity which was paramount for Griffith John was preaching. His advice to fellow-missionaries was, 'Preach, preach, preach.'

Wherever he travelled, preaching was to be carried on in all possible places: on the street, in the chapel, on the bed of a river, or on a boat. In Hankou, the afternoons were spent in preaching, usually from 2 o'clock until 5 or 6 in the evening. Thousands of people would have heard the Christian message as they passed through the street.

The skills, conviction of heart and fervency that had gained him the name of 'The Boy-Preacher' in Wales, and that had set a new example of daily street-preaching to his fellow-missionaries in Shanghai, continued with him throughout his years in Central China. A visitor from Scotland, in 1878, described him preaching to a small group of Westerners in Hankou, and in doing so provides us with a visual picture of Griffith John in his forty-sixth year:

> At first sight he struck me as a man the like of whom one does not meet with every day. Under the average height,

Griffith John's priorities

but strongly built and muscular; a massive head well set on powerful neck; features prominent but regular and pleasing; a flashing eye and a wealth of jet-black hair—he looked the very personification of ability and energy. The sermon he delivered that morning to barely a baker's dozen of Europeans would have crowded the largest church in London.

More typical is the description of an afternoon's work during one of innumerable itinerant journeys from town to town, and village to village. In a remote village more than a hundred miles from Hankou:

> Tung had arranged a platform and benches outside the house as he expected many to attend that day ... Villagers continued to come during the day. If the preacher was not present when they arrived they would call for him to start preaching again. He found it difficult to have a quiet time; if he went to his bedroom, or went for a walk, the people would flock after him wanting to hear a sermon. Indeed they would plead with him to resume preaching ... There was no end to the activity until 10 o'clock in the evening.

A fellow LMS missionary in Hankou who worked beside Griffith John from 1867 to 1884 stated that he had often heard him say that not a single day of the year passed without his proclaiming the evangel either in street or chapel.

The Rev. Joseph Adams of the American Baptist Missionary Union visited Hankou sometime in the late 1890s and published an account of a typical service with John ministering:

> The visitor to the London Mission, Hankou, picks his way

gingerly along the 'Pig Street', avoiding rushing coolies, busy tradespeople, sedan chairs and the puddles. Turning aside into a wide gateway, he sees a large and handsome brick building, enclosed in a compound with high protecting firewalls. A pleasant-looking gate-keeper smiles welcome. You notice the characters, 'Fuh ying huei tang', 'Gospel Meeting Hall', over the doors, and entering the building you are surprised to hear a low hum of voices ... You are before a congregation of six or seven hundred men and women who are waiting for the service to begin ...

We have time to study the congregation to which Dr John is going to preach. Many are aged men and women, old pilgrims to Zion, who soon will see the King in his beauty. There are bright boys with hymn-books and Bibles tied up in their handkerchiefs, looking very important; girls with gay attire, hair tightly braided, and all expectant ...

There is a hush, as a short man, with healthy, bright face, keen eyes, white beard and black hair, comes on the platform ... he bends his head in prayer ... The hymn is announced and a rustle of leaves follows. Then the singing! At first an indistinct roar, it gradually shapes itself into some well-known tune, and all sing with the voice of many waters: not very musical but all in time, swaying to and fro, mouths well open, heads thrown back.

When the sermon comes it is easy to see that the audience expect to listen. There is no settling down in easy corners behind convenient pillars. The converts sit, Testaments open, ready to find the next text or the references, showing by the facility with which they read that they know whether 'Timothy' comes before or after 'Hebrews'. Dr John keeps his Bible in one hand, with a sheet of notepaper containing

Griffith John's priorities

an outline of his sermon; with the forehand of the other hand he enforces his points. Sometimes he forgets his book and notes, and in the fire of his earnestness he speaks with vehemence, pacing to and fro on the platform ...

As one listens to the impassioned words, we notice several things—Dr John's intense sympathy with the brothers and sisters to whom he speaks. They are beloved of his soul, and they know it. We notice too his knowledge of their trials, their persecutions, their stumbling blocks, and a starting tear here and there shows that his beautiful and resonant voice has carried a comforting and softening message right to the heart.

Then comes a change. The speaker is dwelling on sin and its character in the sight of a pure and a holy God. How keen is the analysis of man's self-deception; how scathing the exposure of duplicity, falsehood and cunning; how terrible the picture of the wreck and ruin which are the wages of sin. We forget we are listening in Chinese. We feel the speaker is as grandly eloquent as ever he could be in his native Welsh or his adopted English tongue. The scholars, merchants, working men and women of his audience, listen breathlessly, often giving little expressions of amusement, of distress, of pity, of sorrow, as their feelings are touched in one way or another. What a royal preacher is Griffith John, and how magnificently he has for fifty years revelled in the joy of preaching One who is mighty to save. To God be the glory! How faithfully God, the Holy Spirit, has owned and blessed the plain preaching of the Gospel. There are 'signs following' on every hand.

The following comment by Griffith John is an enduring testimony to the truth that 'after that in the wisdom of

God the world by wisdom knew not God, it pleased God by the foolishness of preaching to save them that believe'. It is as true now, in any part of the world in the twenty-first century, as it was then in Central China at the end of the nineteenth century:

> After thirty-eight years of experience in the mission-field, and having tried various methods of work, I do not hesitate to say that here in Central China the method *par excellence* is the daily heralding of the Gospel in the chapels and the streets. Two candidates for baptism came before us this morning, and both of them have been brought to Christ through daily preaching. Several of the sixty-eight adults who have joined us this year have been brought in through the same instrumentality.
>
> This work cannot be reduced into statistics; and yet it is the work to which I attach most value.

9

A Time of Refreshing (1875)

Remarriage

Margaret John had died in March 1873. Although by nature an optimist, and by grace a man of exceptional faith and trust, yet, at times, Griffith John experienced periods of depression. After his return to China these attacks became more frequent and acute. According to Thompson, 'He was living alone, and though he told his correspondents that he was being well looked after by old and faithful friends, the shadow of his recent great bereavement rested heavily upon him, and was made harder to bear by the weakening effects of dysentery.' He sought relief by giving himself even more fully to the work, but had to confess to a friend that he was very lonely and depressed, and did not know how he could go on. He was rescued from this state by the friendship and then the love of Jeannette Jenkins, the widow of an American missionary with the Methodist Episcopal mission in Shanghai. Since her husband's death in 1871, she had been engaged in superintending schools and visitation among the Chinese women of Shanghai. She and Griffith John were married in October 1874 and, after settling in at Hankou, she soon learnt the local dialect and began to lead the women's work.

Griffith John had noted:

> There are three kinds of work which might be carried on by foreign Christian women at this place, namely, conducting classes for female converts, visiting heathen women at their homes, and superintending schools for girls. These three kinds of work are exceedingly important; and no station can be said to be complete in its organisations, and thoroughly efficient in its operations, where they are wanting. They all lie, however, beyond the sphere of the missionary.

In recent years, these aspects had not been addressed sufficiently because of the state of Margaret's health. The arrival of Jeannette soon brought about a great change in this aspect of the work. Her godliness, abilities and exceptional energy, and the sheer power of her Christian witness, resulted in an increasing number of Chinese women finding the courage to profess conversion and join the church, something that had been rare previously, and in a greater gathering-in of whole Chinese families into the fold. This brought about an increase in the numbers within the mission schools, which again Jeannette was completely capable of organising.

It may be that the exceptionally able character of both his wives was a factor in Griffith John's disagreement with Hudson Taylor as to the wisdom of bringing unmarried women out to the mission field. The work among women,

A Time of Refreshing (1875)

he judged, could be fulfilled by the missionary's wife. 'You will probably conclude from the tone of this letter,' he wrote, in a letter home to the LMS secretary in 1875, 'that I am not a strong believer in unmarried Female Agents for China.' Eventually, impressed by the character and work of the unmarried women being brought out to China by the CIM, his views on this point were to change.

A SEASON OF BLESSING

Jeannette's influence was to benefit Griffith John at a more personal, spiritual level also. After her first husband's death she had known an experience of the Holy Spirit in which 'the Heavenly Dove descended upon her as a spirit of sanctity and power'. Such an experience was exactly what Griffith John was seeking at this point in his life, for his own spiritual growth and, perhaps even more, for power and effect in his missionary work. Some months after his marriage, he also experienced an extraordinary period of blessing. He described it many years later:

> I was eight years old when I joined the Church, I preached my first sermon when I was fourteen, and yet I was a missionary for twenty years before I had a full vision of Christ as an ever-present Saviour from sin. This vision of Christ is absolutely necessary for success.

At the time, writing to Elijah Jacob, he noted:

> I long to be filled with divine knowledge, divine wisdom, divine love, divine holiness, to the utmost extent of my capacity. I want to feel that "all the currents of my soul are interfused in one channel deep and wide, and all flowing towards the heart of Christ". I hardly begin to know what treasures there are for us in Christ. It seems to me that every

one of us might be spiritually and ought to be unspeakably mightier than we are. It is the Holy Ghost in us that is everything, and the Father is willing to bestow Him upon the weakest if he will but ask in the spirit of implicit faith and entire self-surrender. My cry these days is for a Pentecost, first on myself and my missionary brethren, and then on the native Church, and then on the heathen at large.

There are phrases in this letter—'implicit faith' and 'entire self-surrender', for example—that remind us of the 'Higher Christian life' teaching of the Holiness movement, associated in Britain with the teaching of the Keswick Convention. This was certainly a strong element in the beliefs of the CIM and of Hudson Taylor in particular. A few of the LMS missionaries were also affected by it. Griffith John was certainly influenced by it, but he does not seem to have believed in a once-for-all 'second blessing' which would open the door to subsequent 'victorious Christian living'. He seems to interpret this blessing more in terms of the times of revival and refreshing he had experienced in Wales. The 'Pentecost' he sought was one of a quickening of energy and power in the corporate life of the church and its community. This was certainly the immediate effect at the time. His preaching became even more powerful and direct, with a greater expectation of immediate conviction and conversion, and almost immediately a difference was felt in the life of the church.

Griffith John decided to hold daily prayer meetings for a week. Noel Gibbard describes the results:

> The Chinese were not easily moved to tears, but in these meetings the whole congregation cried and groaned under the guilt of sin, and this turned to rejoicing in salvation.

A Time of Refreshing (1875)

Prayer continued for long periods without interruption, people crying to God for the conversion of individuals and families. Griffith John had not seen anything like it in China, and was reminded of revival meetings in Wales.

One of the most important addresses that Griffith John ever delivered in China was that on 'The Holy Spirit in connection with Mission Work', presented at the 1877 Shanghai Conference (see chapter 12), and the convictions then expressed derived from his experiences at this time.

10
THE SPRINGBOARD TO CENTRAL CHINA (1871–85)

Although the Tsientin Treaty of 1860 had opened up the land, the various missionary societies had been very slow to respond to the new circumstances. They were realistic in realising that a statement promising free passage and security promulgated in Beijing might be interpreted and carried out very differently in the semi-independent provinces hundreds of miles away from the capital. But no great progress was being made. A. J. Broomhall describes the general situation at the time:

> The coastal treaty ports were still a cage confining the missionary bodies. Since the first historic deployment of a handful of waiting pioneers, after the unequal treaties of 1842–4, missionaries had been restricted to those ports, unless they took risks. The notable few were the exceptions to the rule. For seventeen years, from 1843–60, at an

immense price in life and health, the majority had studied China and the Chinese, translated the Scriptures and books of science and law, conducted their schools and preached their hearts out, with scant results in terms of converts and churches ... The CMS began work in Fujian in 1850 and ten years later reported seeing no interest being shown in the message, 'no visible results, no converts to the truth, no baptisms' ...

Conspicuous in the reports and reviews of the *Chinese Recorder* was the inability of society after society in place after place to report activities under the title of 'itinerancy' or 'itineration'. Few attempted anything resembling the extensive travels of Burdon, Muirhead, Griffith John, William Aitchison, William Burns, Hudson Taylor and others. The Bible Society representatives and colporteurs were outstanding in their achievement, following the pattern set by Alexander Wylie in 1863. Most mission stations were static, looking to local growth for future expansion throughout China.

The exploration by Griffith John and Alexander Wylie of the Yangzi River, their penetration into Sichuan and northwards into Shaanxi, and other similar shorter forays, were not intended as mere geographical expeditions, even though they were the means of greatly increasing Western knowledge of these foreign regions. The overriding purpose was to find out to what extent missionaries might safely travel with the gospel as the country began to open up. The two men were placing themselves as guinea pigs in repeated experiments to discover where missionaries might be expected to be attacked by the mob, beaten up, in danger of death, or where the 'foreign devils' would be tolerated, or even be allowed to stay. Griffith

The springboard to Central China (1871–85)

John experienced all these possibilities many times. If it was argued that he was foolishly and sinfully exposing himself to danger and risking his life, he would reply that the *status quo* was not an option. If all remained safely in their missionary communities and well-established preaching stations, the gospel would not prosper. There had to be pioneers to blaze the trail for there to be any possibility of others following. He fully hoped that he himself would be following up his initial visits for years to come; but if, instead, he proved to be a martyr, this was all in God's hands. The possibility of his death did not alter the necessity for such pioneering attempts.

AN ENFORCED CHANGE OF APPROACH

Griffith John's itinerating zeal, however, eventually came into conflict with LMS policy as a result of the Yangzhou riots in 1868. Hudson Taylor had rented a house in the town of Yangzhou, south-west of Shanghai, in order to establish a CIM mission-station. A rioting mob set fire to the house and drove out the occupants (including Hudson Taylor and his wife) who, until they were rescued by the local magistrate's forces, were in very real danger of losing their lives. Although Hudson Taylor had not requested help at the time, the British consul became involved and the events were taken up by the British Press, discussed in the Houses of Parliament, and led to a reaction against the activities of the missionaries by sectors of the British government more interested in commercial and mercantile interests. Influenced by this reaction, the LMS issued instructions that all their missionaries should withdraw to the treaty ports and confine their activities to those of pre-Peking Treaty days. This was completely unacceptable to Griffith John. He refused to leave Hankou, arguing that to retreat would be to set back the work of the gospel for years. Wardlaw Thompson, his biographer, commented, 'When the spirit of the pioneer is dead, the Christian Society which has to record the fact begins to write its own epitaph.'

Eventually the LMS backed down and agreed to maintain the Hankou station; but this victory came at a cost. From now on Griffith John had to put aside many of his plans for itinerating and planting far-flung stations. In particular, his hopes of a mission at Chengdu in Sichuan were dissolved and it would be twenty years before an LMS church was formed in that province. His practice of short evangelistic journeys of two or three weeks into the regions of Hubei continued, however, throughout the whole of his life. Many times a year he would depart from Hankou, saying his farewells to Margaret or, later, Jeannette, leaving them not knowing whether they would ever see their husband again. Travelling on foot, by boat up the Han or the Yangzi rivers, by sedan chair, or even, in later years, by railway train, he would arrive at a new town or village, walk into the nearest street and raise his voice to the crowd that always gathered to view 'the foreign devils' and preach to them Jesus Christ, crucified. The many millions of the Chinese peoples ensured that there were always 'regions beyond' to visit. He reviewed a year's journeys in the late 1860s:

> An unusual amount of itinerating work has been done this year ... Some walled cities and many unwalled towns and villages have been visited by us on these tours. Copies of the word of God have been extensively sold, and the Gospel has been widely preached. Our work was carried on sometimes on the road, sometimes in the streets, and sometimes in the temples. Many of these places had never been visited before

by any foreigner, and at none of them, so far as we could learn, had the Gospel been preached ... A certain amount of itineration ought to be done yearly in connection with every station. Its reflex influence on both the missionary and the mission is most healthful and stimulating. It tends to enlarge the ideas, deepen the longings, intensify the ardour, and brace up the nerves of both pastor and people. One often feels at the end of a hundred or two hundred miles' tour, having spent a fortnight or three weeks in preaching from town to town and village to village, that he could dare anything and endure anything.

A STRONG BASE IN HUBEI

The focused concentration of Griffith John's organising abilities on the establishing and expansion of a stronghold of Christian witness, however, bore much fruit. By 1875 the church in Hankou had registered 353 baptised adults. Ten years later this had risen to 777. Such a strong church provided a 'nucleus of an aggressive and extensive missionary penetration into the surrounding provinces'. It acted as a stepping-stone: welcoming other workers, helping them to acclimatise in Central China, to improve their language skills and to learn of the local culture, before proceeding onwards to 'regions beyond', westwards and northwards. To these eager itinerants, Hankou could act in much the same way as Shanghai had done for Griffith John during his five years' residence there: nurturing his emerging skills before releasing him to the west.

As the years passed, Griffith John began to appreciate, more and more, the advantages that the strong Hankou base provided. During his visit to Britain in 1872 he made the comment that the scope he had in his Hankou field was greater than Spurgeon's in London. This was no exaggeration. The population of the Wuhan metropolis at the time was probably something over four million, as compared to the three and a half million inhabitants of London, but the gospel stations set as lights on a hill before these four million comprised only two or three mission churches together with their outlying preaching stations, compared with the hundreds of other churches and chapels of London that shared together in the gospel work with the Metropolitan Tabernacle. Furthermore, for a radius of many hundreds of miles around Wuhan, lived the teeming millions of three provinces, Hubei, Henan and Hunan, among which there existed at the time no more than a few hundred believers.

Representatives of other societies at Hankou

The provision of a helping hand was one of the many contributions of the Hankou church during the next forty years. Indeed Griffith John had acted in this way almost from his very arrival at the city.

Alexander Wylie, John's companion on the exploration of the upper Yangzi, was an LMS co-worker, but from 1863 he was a representative of the British and Foreign Bible Society. A major motivation for their epic journey together in 1868 was the understanding of the need for extensive distribution of the Scriptures in Chinese. In so many places where the preached Word had not or could not enter, the written Word could still convict and convert. During his later years in China, Wylie worked in every port where missions had been established and visited twelve of the country's eighteen provinces.

The springboard to Central China (1871–85)

In 1862 Griffith John invited Josiah Cox of the Wesleyan Methodist Missionary Society from Canton to Hankou. With his encouragement Cox undertook preaching itineraries, firstly up the Yangzi to Chichuan and then venturing as the first Protestant missionary to Changsha in the antagonistic Hunan province, meeting much resistance.

In 1865, W. Scarborough and David Hill, both Methodists, joined him. Scarborough's journey up the Han River to Guanghua was the longest undertaken since that of John and Wylie. David Hill (1840–1896) established a station at nearby Wuchang. One of the Hankou converts, Chu Shao An, was allocated to him as a language teacher and was eventually, in 1880, to become a Methodist minister at Wuchang. In 1878, David Hill travelled to south Shanxi to help in the aid effort in the wake of the tragic famine of that year. He estimated that three-quarters of the region had perished in the famine. Nine and a half million died in the four provinces of Shanxi, Zhili, Henan and Shandong. David Hill returned to Wuchang in 1879, but not before he was instrumental in the conversion of Hsi Shengmo, whose remarkable life is so well-known from the biography *Pastor Hsi* by Geraldine Taylor.

In 1868 a representative of the National Bible Society of Scotland, named Oxenham, became the first to visit Hankou from the north, having travelled over seven hundred miles from Beijing. In that year also a representative of the American Episcopal Protestant Church established a mission at Hankou. In this one case, however, an example of 'sheep-stealing', compounded by not informing Griffith John, made co-operation difficult.

The China Inland Mission, following the godly leadership

of Hudson Taylor, had never retreated from its policy of itinerating, and Griffith John always rejoiced at opportunities to help the mission. A. J. Broomhall, the CIM historian, comments: 'Only loyalty to his mission board prevented Griffith John from adding Chonqing or Chengdu to Wuhan as his bases for intensive church-planting. So he supported CIM to the hilt.' The CIM's first missionary in the region was M. Henry Taylor. He had been designated to enter the province of Henan, north of Hubei, where few Westerners had ventured. A Chinese Christian from the Wuchang church was assigned to him and together they left Hankou on 3 April 1875. They arrived back fifty-six days later, having preached the gospel and sold Scriptures in this gospel-less province. In the autumn, they returned for a further eighty-four days' itinerary. On this second journey, 'they found four believers standing firm, the first-fruits of the Church of millions in Henan today'.

However, even in the case of his closest allies, he did not open his doors without careful thought of the consequences and judging each case by its merits. Thus, when Hudson Taylor visited him in 1874 with the suggestion of establishing a CIM station at Hankou, his initial response was lukewarm.

> Griffith John invited him to move in and stay, although not understanding, yet, why a fourth mission should be added to the LMS, WMMF and Protestant Episcopal Church in the three cities now forming the metropolis of Wuhan. 'I think that the Wesleyan missionaries will be good friends to us,' Hudson Taylor [wrote] ... 'The LMS not *quite* so warm, perhaps, but they see the need of a place here, *if* we are to go beyond'—which was his intention.

The springboard to Central China (1871–85)

Griffith John's own itinerating did not, by any means, come to an end in 1868, as we shall see in later chapters. His tours were merely reduced in number and distance. But for the cases mentioned above, and for so many others, the nature and position of Griffith John's extended church at Hankou and Wuchang was the catalyst for the hopes, plans and achievements of many brave expeditions by preachers of the Word. In ever increasing numbers as the century drew to its close, missionaries would be helped on their way from Hankou, prepared and equipped, and then welcomed back, provided with rest and recuperation, and their tales of success and opposition listened to with avid interest.

OTHER VISITORS

A remarkable feature of Griffith John's leadership during his many years in China was his knowledge of contemporary trends and movements within Christian missionary circles; not only those within the various provinces of China, but also in the outside world. This knowledge was predominantly obtained through the many periodicals that arrived at Hankou, but another important source was the information gleaned from the many visitors that passed through the city. A few examples of his responses to news items and to various visitors reveal his own views and judgements as he encountered the issues of the day.

In July 1888, he received an account of the Congregational Union of England and Wales annual May meetings, and wrote to thank his correspondent:

> Thank you very much for sending me the special numbers of The Christian World; also for the Pall Mall and other

papers which you send me from time to time. I have read with a good deal of interest much of what the special numbers contain. What a wonderful month your May is. Is there anything like it in any part of the world? It strikes me that the spiritual element in them is not very strong. Man is very visible in them, but is the presence of God much felt? You are in a better position to judge. In reading the addresses and speeches I cannot but see and feel the ability, cleverness, and earnestness of many of the speakers and readers; but I feel that something real is lacking.

One visit, whose aftermath would have left an indelible impression upon Griffith John, occurred very early on in his residence at Hankou. In March 1864 a young LMS missionary—Robert Jerman Thomas (1840–1866)—was sent from Shanghai to Hankou to gain experience in the field. There were many reasons why Griffith John would have been the ideal mentor for Robert Thomas. The young man's father (Robert Thomas, senior) had trained for the ministry at Brecon Congregational College, like Griffith John, leaving there sixteen years before him. He then settled in Swansea, at Shiloh Welsh Congregational Chapel, Landore, less than two miles from Ebenezer. He was pastor there from 1837 to 1839: the three years leading up to Griffith John's ninth birthday. As the pastor of the nearest church in the denomination, he would no doubt have been a familiar figure to the Ebenezer congregation. His name became well-known to the whole denomination after his move to Rhayader Congregational Chapel in 1840 because a remarkable revival broke out under his ministry, with over a hundred new members being accepted into the church in 1841. Robert Jerman Thomas was born in Rhayader in 1840 and was nine years younger than Griffith

John. In 1847 he moved with his family when his father was called to Hanover Chapel, a Congregational cause at Llanover, south of Abergavenny. It was here, in June 1863, that he was ordained to the work of a missionary with the LMS. He had recently married Caroline Godfrey from Northampton, and they sailed for Shanghai a month after the ordination, arriving there eight years after Griffith John.

When Robert arrived in Hankou, Griffith John must have been struck by the similarities between them, in their national and cultural backgrounds and in their personal lives. The news that he would hear in the following years concerning his young friend must have saddened him greatly. Robert returned to Shanghai from Hankou only to find that his pregnant wife had given birth prematurely while he was away and that both Caroline and the baby had died. His health suffered to such an extent that he resigned from his LMS work and took up a government post. During 1865 he made a long journey through the west coast region of Korea, becoming the first Protestant Christian to visit that country for an extended period. He learnt that educated Koreans could read Chinese Mandarin script. Resolving to return to the country with Mandarin Bibles, he rejoined the LMS and found an American trading ship, the *General Sherman*, about to cross the Yellow Sea, whose captain agreed to take him with them as an interpreter. The subsequent tragic history of this journey is well-known, ending with the death of Robert Thomas in the act of pressing the Word of God into the hands of those who were clubbing him to death. God's blessing upon these few Bibles, together with others that he had succeeded in distributing in riverside villages as his ship sailed up the Taedong River towards Pyongyang, marked the beginnings of the Christian church in Korea, and Robert Thomas became the first of the very many Christian martyrs who have suffered and died for their faith in Korea.

In July 1864, John Livingston Nevius (1832–93) of the American Presbyterian Mission and his wife, Helen, arrived for a stay at Hankou. They had been ten years in China and had established many stations in the Shandong province. Later they would be heavily involved in aid work during the Great North China Famine of 1877–78. Throughout this time, from the late 60s onwards, Nevius was questioning the missionary methods of the time and developing his 'indigenous church' policy in which missionaries should work towards 'self-propagating, self-governing, and self-supporting' local Chinese churches. He called for the discarding of old-style missions and the adoption of his new plan in order to foster an independent, self-supporting indigenous church. These principles became known as the *Nevius Plan*. Although they never became generally popular in China (with the strong exception of the CIM), they were eagerly embraced by American missionaries in Korea from 1890 onwards, and were to be the principles that underlay the extensive church growth in that country.

In 1885, George Müller, the well-known founder of the orphanage in Bristol and one of the leaders of the Open Brethren, came to Hankou during a lengthy tour of the country. Griffith John wrote his impressions:

> We have just had a visit from George Müller of Bristol. He is a very remarkable man in many ways. He preached once on Saturday, twice on Sunday, and twice on Monday. When leaving on Monday night he told me that he was

not feeling at all tired; yet he is eighty-two years old ... On Monday morning his address to the missionaries was long and impressive. We cannot soon forget the visit. In George Müller our ideal of what a Christian man should be seems to have found a striking realisation.

With other visitors of the same year there was a more critical response. The well-known 'Cambridge Seven' arrived in Shanghai in March 1885. These were seven Cambridge graduates converted as a result of the 1882 Moody and Sankey mission at the university and accepted by the CIM for service in China. One of them, Dixon Hoste, was eventually to become Hudson Taylor's successor and lead the CIM for thirty years. Another, the famous cricketer C. T. Studd, would later serve in India and Africa and become the founder of the World Evangelization Crusade (WEC) missionary society. After a period in Shanghai, Hudson Taylor divided them into two groups. He sent C. T. Studd and the two brothers, Arthur and Cecil Polhill-Turner, to Hankou to be the guests of Griffith John for some days. Writing later of the circumstances of their arrival in China, the latter commented:

> The way these men have been honoured because of their social position and the capital made by the mission out of their names and fame strikes me as something that Paul would have looked upon with great contempt, and Christ would have condemned as unworthy of himself and his cause.

Nor had he been impressed by their intellectual ability. His views are described by Noel Gibbard:

> The Welshman had met three of the seven, and would not

hesitate to say that in point of ability and education not a few in the LMS would be superior to them. C. T. Studd had spent a few days with him, and John believed him to be 'a most lovable man, and thoroughly consecrated'. He was not, however, of great mental capacity or profound erudition. The LMS missionary was sorry that he had not met Stanley Smith who, according to reports received, was 'the finest thinker among them'. The consideration of social standing was not of primary importance. 'All we want are capable men and consecrated men come they from any class they may be.'

The 'last province'

By 1874, nine of China's eighteen provinces had Protestant missions established within them, yet their total efforts were hardly to be compared to the work of Roman Catholic missionaries (Jesuits and Franciscans) in China. These had had the great advantage of over 500 years of familiarity with the land and its people, since the days of Marco Polo, and over 300 years of a Catholic-believing native church since the labours of Francis Xavier. They were to be found throughout China. By contrast, in 1874, there were only 436 Protestant missionaries in the whole country; half of them were women, and the great majority of them, male and female, were still in the coastal provinces. In the next twenty-five years, the situation was completely changed. The strength of the LMS church in Hankou had opened up the Hubei province, and provided the springboard for other societies to advance into Henan and Shanxi to the north. Griffith John's journey with Alexander Wylie had opened up the possibilities of stations in Sichuan and Shaanxi in the west. James Gilmour's travels in the north of the country for the LMS, and the rapid spreading of Hudson Taylor's missionaries to all parts (by 1895, the

The springboard to Central China (1871–85)

CIM alone had 630 personnel in the field), had resulted in province after province being occupied. By 1898, Griffith John could have travelled 1,000 miles or so to the west, or to the north of Hankou, or the 600 miles to the eastern coast, and found a missionary station where he could stay; but had he travelled south a mere seventy miles, into the province of Hunan, he would not have found a place even for a foothold. He, and others, had tried many times, but had always been driven back: such was the conservative, anti-foreign, nationalistic fervour of its population. A Chinese proverb declared that 'Hubei men are made of bean curd, but the Hunan men are made of iron'. Hunan became known as 'the last province', and was the subject of increasing prayer.

11

JAMES HUDSON TAYLOR AND TIMOTHY RICHARD

By 1877 Griffith John was forty-six years old and had been in China for twenty-two years. He was increasingly being looked to by many within the Protestant missionary community in the land for guidance and advice regarding the very many complex and difficult circumstances that faced them. He was soon to make a very definite stand against some of the newer ideas that were being advocated. His own principles are perhaps best illustrated by describing his very different relationships with two other prominent Chinese missionaries. The first, an Englishman, was his closest ally outside the LMS community; the second, ironically a fellow-Welshman, was perhaps his main adversary.

GRIFFITH JOHN, HUDSON TAYLOR AND THE CIM

As mentioned already, one of the very first consequences of John's arrival in China was the eviction of the former tenant of his LMS lodgings to make way for him. This did not in any way affect what developed into a fifty-year friendship. Each greatly admired and respected the other. There is no opportunity in this book to describe the wonderful life and achievements of James Hudson Taylor (1832–1905), the founder of the China Inland Mission (CIM). A year younger than John, he arrived in China two years before him under the auspices of the China Evangelisation Society; but differences of opinion as to the methods by which missionary work should be carried out led to his resigning in 1857 and returning to England. He published the influential book *China: its spiritual needs and claims* in 1865 and returned to the land in 1866 as leader of the newly-formed CIM, with fifteen other missionaries and with decided views on how to proceed. His views differed from the established practices of the three main missions, the LMS, the (Anglican) Church Missionary Society (CMS) and the Baptist Missionary Society (BMS), on four points particularly:

1. The adopting of Chinese dress and the 'queue' (pigtail) when in the interior.

2. The direction of the mission from the field rather than from home.

3. The acceptance of those of limited education, should they show the necessary character for missionary work.

4. An emphasis on itinerancy for the preaching of the gospel and church planting.

With the last three of these points, within the bounds set upon him by his membership of the LMS, Griffith John was in broad agreement, and he became one of the main champions from within the established missionary community of the CIM methods.

The LMS policy was of first establishing a central missionary station (such as Hankou) and then widening the sphere of preaching and church planting in that geographical area. A considerable number of missionaries, a community in fact, would then be based at the station, and medical and educational facilities would evolve as the work was established. In John's first years at Hankou, as we have seen, he itinerated widely. Indeed, his many journeys and the Yangzi expedition comprised far greater travels even than those carried out by Hudson Taylor. This was his preferred method of evangelising. But in compliance with his society's aims he recognised the importance of his presence at Hankou, and he had settled upon a directorial role at the city, combined with frequent forays undertaken to visit the far-flung preaching stations.

His pioneering spirit rejoiced, therefore, as his church was enabled to encourage the young CIM workers on their way as they passed through Hankou. He came to know very many of them. He saw in them and in their director an antidote against the new ethos that was emerging in some of the missionary circles. A. J. Broomhall has described these new ideas:

> Common in the thinking and writing of many of the missionaries over the years had been the transformation of all China by a 'Christianising' process involving cultural changes. The 'literati' were the chief objects of such missionary efforts along intellectual paths. Hudson Taylor saw the same and greater spiritual results arising from direct preaching of the gospel, while Christianising could leave

men's hearts unregenerate. Valuing the work of others, and sometimes contributing to it, he and the CIM were called to share with William Muirhead and Griffith John of the LMS, John Burdon of the CMS and John Nevius the Presbyterian, as evangelists and church planters.

With hindsight, it may be seen that the success and increase of the Chinese Church during its 'open century' from 1840 to 1940 resulted from the combination of strong strategic centres with the itinerating to every corner of the land with the preaching of the Word; but at the time Hudson Taylor was criticised fiercely. Time and again, Griffith John's voice was raised, defending the CIM before his fellow-missionaries. During the 1877 Shanghai Conference, when it was suggested that the CIM were sending out unworthy representatives into the field, John immediately rose to his feet:

> It has been my privilege to come in close contact with not a few missionaries of the China Inland Mission ... Some of them are well-educated, having received college or university training; and by far the majority of those among them who have received only a fair English education, are men of real character and great worth. Some of them speak the language with as much correctness, fluency and fullness as any missionary in China ... Many appear to be as fit for pastoral work as the majority of their more highly educated brethren ... A man is not an *inferior* man because he has not had a college training; whilst a man may be a very inferior *missionary* in spite of the highest educational advantages.

As Taylor's base was at Hangzhou, south of Shanghai, and as he was away from China often, travelling as director of his society, he and John saw each other very rarely during their fifty years of friendship.

TIMOTHY RICHARD

Timothy Richard (1845–1919) was born in the small village of Ffaldybrenin, Carmarthenshire, Wales. Deeply affected by the 1859 Revival, he applied to the CIM to work as a missionary in China. The CIM suggested that he work with his own denomination's society, the BMS. In this way he arrived at Shanghai in 1870 and was sent to the northern province of Shandong. This was some 600 miles from Hankou, and he and Griffith John met one another only on a handful of occasions. He spent his first years in language learning and itinerant preaching, but his experience was very different from that of Griffith John.

> I did not find the preaching very productive of good results and was consequently considerably discouraged ... In my evangelistic work during the first two years in Chefoo (Yentai) I had tried street-chapel preaching without any success worth mentioning. I then began to follow the plan of "seeking the worthy" as our Lord commanded, for I found that they constituted the "good ground" in which to sow the seed.

The reference here is to Matthew 10:11, 'And into whatsover city or town ye shall enter, enquire who in it is worthy; and there abide till ye go thence.' Richard would seek out those considered devout and learned men in the towns he visited and engage them in discussion on religious topics. He began to study the Chinese classics and Eastern religions and then to publish tracts and pamphlets emphasizing not so much the unique claims of Christianity as the ethical and moral concepts that are common to

Christianity, Confucianism and Buddhism. In this way he hoped to win the trust of this class of men and then lead them on to Christianity.

Up to this point the differences between Griffith John and Richard may be accepted as the different approaches of the evangelistic preacher and the apologist—each contending in their different ways for the same faith. But Richard began to move away from the orthodox faith, particularly after 1876, when a severe famine developed in the northern provinces. Some have suggested that this was the worst famine the world had known. Between 15 and 20 million Chinese died. Richard manifested such remarkable administrative skills as he sought to alleviate the disaster that he was appointed by the Missionary Societies Joint Aid Council to supervise their work in the Shanxi province, where the famine was greatest. This experience affected him greatly. He recognised that the ignorant and obscurantist attitude of the Qing dynasty and the provincial leaders, in their determination to refuse every Western influence, was depriving the land of all advances in medicine, education, industry and transport. He felt increasingly the challenge to rescue the pagan not only from the sufferings of the world to come but from those of the present world. Influence had to be brought to bear upon these leaders in order to save the nation. 'I wish to gain the leaders,' he said. 'If you have the leaders, the rest will follow.'

MISSIONARY TENSIONS

Up until this time Richard had been collaborating with the CIM missionaries in Shanxi. At one time Jennie Taylor, Hudson Taylor's wife, had lodged in his residence. But his strength of character and his strong views began to affect some of his CIM and BMS co-workers. The term 'Shanxi Spirit' was minted to describe the decline and lack of evangelistic zeal that would manifest itself in some of the missionaries sent there. Hudson Taylor wrote in 1878:

> The faith of one brother has quite broken down under the unhelpful influence largely of other missionaries and we shall have to recall him.

He continued, referring to Richard and to two CIM workers who had come under his influence:

> His presence in Shanxi causes me great anxiety for some of his views are so Romish, and his personal influence so strong that the CIM has no existence, scarcely, or place, or work or claims in the minds of two of the CIM missionaries. This is not necessarily Mr R's fault; it is rather the inevitable result of a strong and attractive character over weaker minds.

The two men were so convinced of the rightness of Richard's policy that the persistence of the rest of the Shanxi team in their scriptural colportage and evangelism was pushing them towards resignation from the society. Taylor commented further:

> Richard is driving a good theory to death. He refuses to preach to the masses, is for circulation of moral and theistic tracts, not containing the name or work of Christ, to prepare the way as he thinks for the gospel.

The result was that the CIM refused to collaborate further with Timothy Richard, drawing an end to four years of disagreement and weariness of spirit.

Richard now began to urge the BMS to establish colleges

in every province in order to provide Western education. The BMS refused to do this, arguing that their supporting churches would not allow them to use their money in that way. Richard therefore resigned from the society and worked as a journalist for the most influential periodical in the north, the monthly *Wan Guo Gong Bao* or *Review of the Times*, which Young Allen had founded in 1868. His many articles emphasized the practical applications of the Christian faith and portrayed Christianity as a useful concept for the Chinese, comparable to other ideas such as market economics and international law. It was Christianity that had provided the education and culture in the West that brought forth such knowledge of the laws of God in nature. This knowledge had subsequently released all the miracles of science and technology. It was therefore the responsibility of Christian missionaries to present these Christian blessings to the Chinese. If not to all, if not to the peasantry of town and village, then to the leaders, so that the country might be 'Christianised' and saved by their influence.

At the periodical's offices in Tianjin, Richard was close to the government in Beijing, and he was often at meetings with ministers and advisers. In 1891 he was appointed general secretary of the SPCK in China and spent the next twenty-five years of his life producing literature aimed in particular at the 'literati' of the country. Throughout these years, he was one of the strongest voices calling for reform in China. When the Qing dynasty finally fell in 1911, most of the pro-reform leaders of the new republic—Sun Yat Sen, the first prime minister, in particular—were men who had been strongly influenced by his philosophy.

12

THE SHANGHAI MISSIONARY CONFERENCES (1877, 1890 AND 1907)

Because of the diverging views among the evangelical missionaries in areas such as methodology, culture, and even theology, the fear arose that in some aspects of the work they might find themselves at cross purposes. In order to help one another and to arrive at some consensus a general conference was arranged for all the Protestant missionary organisations. The first of these gatherings, known as the Shanghai Missionary Conferences, was held in 1877. Griffith John, Hudson Taylor and twenty-five other delegates had met at Wuchang earlier in the year to organise the conference and draw up its programme. It was convened on 10 May and lasted until 24 May. 126 delegates from twenty societies, and many countries, were present. Timothy Richard had only been in China for eight years at this point and was not therefore one of the invited speakers, but there were others who held to the same convictions. Two of these, the eminent American Presbyterian missionary, William A. P. Martin (1827–1916), who was to spend fifty-seven years in China, and Young Allen argued the case that secular and scientific literature would be of greater value in undermining Chinese superstition than evangelistic tracts. The two main speakers who opposed their views and, in doing so, expressed the majority opinion, were Griffith John and Hudson Taylor.

The titles of the addresses delivered at the conference reflect the orthodoxy of the majority present: 'Preaching the gospel to every creature', 'Our field of labour', 'Methods of preaching', 'Itinerating preaching' (an address given by Hudson Taylor), 'The relationship between the churches'. Griffith John spoke very fully in many of the debates: Buddhism and Taoism; preaching; medical missions; Christian literature; the elevation of the native Church; the opium question; systematic cooperation among societies; and other topics.

An important address

The title of John's main address at the conference reveals, very clearly, his vision of missionary work: 'The Holy Spirit and his relationship to Mission'. It was based on Luke 11:13, 'If ye then, being evil, know how to give good gifts unto your children: how much more shall your heavenly Father give the Holy Spirit to them that ask him?' He noted:

> We are in China in obedience to the command of our Lord; the purpose of our mission is to disciple and make Christians of this great nation ...

This is spiritual work, and to secure success in it we need the abiding presence of the Spirit, and through the Spirit such a full baptism of power as will perfectly fit each one of us for the special work which God has given him to do.

1. *The Spirit is the source of all spiritual illumination.* Knowledge, even religious knowledge, without spiritual illumination is of the letter, and its possession brings no spiritual power. 'The things of God' as facts and doctrines are fully revealed in this blessed Book ... Still the Bible is not enough for us. The vital question is, how are we to *know* 'the things that are freely given us of God'? ...

Then look at our converts. The ease with which many of them acquire knowledge of the facts and doctrines of the Bible is simply astonishing. But where is the missionary who does not lament the lack of *spiritual* discernment on the part of the great bulk of his converts? The truths that are lodged in their intellects, and which they accept as unquestionable verities, do not appear to move them deeply. Their spiritual nature is not intensely quickened and greatly expanded by 'the things of the Spirit of God', neither are their moral activities powerfully energised by them. They lack that divinely illumined, soul-transforming apprehension of spiritual truth essential to the development of a strong, manly, noble Christian character.

2. *The Holy Spirit is the immediate source of all holiness.* The missionary must be above all things a holy man. The ideal teacher of the Chinese is a holy man:

"He is entirely sincere, and perfect in love. He is magnanimous, generous, benign, and full of forbearance. He is pure in heart, free from selfishness, and never swerves from the path of duty in his conduct. He is deep and active like a fountain, sending forth his virtues in due season. He is seen, and men revere him; he speaks, and men believe him; he acts, and men are gladdened by him. He possesses all heavenly virtues. He is one with Heaven."

This is a lofty ideal ... and I am convinced that no Christian teacher in China can be a *great spiritual* power in whom this ideal is not embodied and manifested in an eminent degree ... He must be a man full of the Holy Ghost, and the divinity within him must energise mightily through him. He must be a man who will take time, not only to master the language and literature of this people, but to be holy. It is not ourselves—our poor selves—the Chinese want to see, but God in us.

3. *The Holy Spirit is the source of spiritual unity.*

4. *He is the Fount of all true joy.* We as missionaries need the fullness of this joy. Without it our work will be a burden to us, and we shall toil on with the hearts of slaves; and the hearts of slaves are never strong. But especially do our native brethren need it. They had their pleasures in their heathen condition, both religious and sensuous. We have taken these away from them. How are they to be kept from falling a-lusting for the flesh-pots of Egypt—for the leeks and onions and garlic of their pagan life? There can only be one way; the new religion must be made a joy to them.

5. *The Holy Spirit is the source of power in dealing with souls.*

6. *He is the inspirer of all true prayer.*

He concluded by discussing three questions:

(a) Are we and our converts *filled* with the Holy Ghost?

(b) Is a new Pentecost possible?

(c) How is the fullness of the Spirit to be obtained?

The address ended with the following words:

I want to return from this Conference, not only stimulated in mind and enriched with a store of valuable information, but filled with the Holy Ghost. China is *dead—terribly* dead. Our plans and organisations can do very little for this great people. They want Life ... The secret of the success of the Apostles lay not in what they did or said, but in the presence of Christ in them and with them. They saw with the eyes of Christ, felt with his heart, and worked with his energies. They were nothing; Christ was everything ... They spake with the demonstration of the Spirit; when they came into contact with men, a mysterious energy went out of them and under their vitalising touch dead souls started into life ... Brethren, this is what we must be, if this mighty Empire is to be moved through us. But to be this, the throne of grace must be our refuge—the secret place of the Most High must be our daily and hourly habitation. We must *take time* to become filled with his power; we must *take time* to be *holy.* Let us put our desires into one heart-felt petition for a baptism of the Holy Ghost, and not cease to present it until we have prevailed. So Elijah prayed; he threw himself on the ground, resolved not to rise till his request was granted. So Jacob WRESTLED with the angel. So Daniel set his face unto the Lord his God. So the disciples continued with one accord in prayer and supplication.

Griffith John's assessment of the greatest need of the church and of the answer to that need is as relevant today as it has ever been throughout the Christian centuries.

Two further quotations from this address reveal what was to be his consistent response to the differing viewpoints being expressed:

> We are here not to develop the resources of the country, not for the advancement of civilisation; but to do battle with the powers of darkness, to save men from sin, and conquer China for Christ.
>
> Social regeneration, even national education, could do little until a spiritual regeneration had taken place.

THE 1890 AND 1907 CONFERENCES

Griffith John does not seem to have been present at the second Shanghai Conference in 1890. Timothy Richard was present and taking a prominent role. His main responsibility was to support William Martin as the latter argued for tolerance from the missionaries towards the old Chinese practice of worshipping or, at the very least, giving undue homage to the spirits of their ancestors. At this conference, again, it was the viewpoint of the orthodox majority that prevailed. The title of Timothy Richard's second address, 'The Relationship between Christian Mission and the Chinese Government', reveals the avenue by means of which Christian progress was to be found, as he believed.

By the third Shanghai General Conference of 1907, Hudson Taylor had died and Griffith John was suffering from the effects of his first stroke. The focus on education, culture, organisation and ecumenism had now clearly taken the place of any emphasis on the gospel (except that some societies such as the CIM were worthy exceptions). A. J. Broomhall summarises Richard's presentation at this time:

He gave a long discourse on "How few men may make a million converts". Because one soul is more valuable than the whole world and many were open to adopting a new religion, he reasoned, while the Student Volunteer Movement was aiming at no less than the evangelisation of the world in this generation, an acceptable gospel offered in an acceptable form could see millions accepting it. Change mission methods and change the appearance of the gospel. So he summarised the leading religions of the world to show features they had in common.

One of them, Christianity, he sub-divided. Early Christianity had higher ideals than Judaism and other religions. By making God universal instead of merely national, by substituting faith for old ritual, and higher ethics for lower, by mystic union with God and consequent immortality, Christianity was an advance on other religions. But 'Reformed Christianity' still higher than Early Christianity, he claimed, was conquering the world by substituting individual liberty of conscience for papal authority, by improved education, by letting the people have more voice in government, by enlightened uplifting of all nations and races—still with no mention of Christ. The religions of the world must be studied for the power of the Holy Spirit is believed in by them all. Not that they use our phraseology but they have the same ideas.

When the missionary has given an outline of the material, social, intellectual and religious advantages and has persevered till they thoroughly understand, then the conversion of China will be accomplished as suddenly as the explosion of a mine. Why should we follow antiquated methods of mission work when the new produces results a thousand times better?

Such was the core question of Timothy Richard's philosophy by 1907. The gulf between his thought and that of Hudson Taylor and Griffith John had become unbridgeable. *The Cambridge History of China* comments that this teaching '[met with] massive unresponsiveness … The message [they] finally succeeded in conveying to Chinese of prominence turned out to be secular rather than religious in content.' It is startling, and very sad, that a man who was inspired to give himself to the mission field by the powerful authentic work of the Holy Spirit in the 1859 Revival in Wales should end up maintaining such a sterile, Christ-dishonouring position.

13

HOME AGAIN (1880)

In 1879, Griffith John wrote to Wardlaw Thompson in London:

I have received a letter from Griffith, David and Mary today, and the burden of the whole is 'Come home'. My dear friend, my mind is much burdened and saddened as I write this. The impulse of the heart is decidedly Wales-ward. But how can I leave my work? If I am anything at all, I am a missionary. I am a missionary, not in profession, but in heart and soul. In regard to the work, necessity is laid upon me, and woe be unto me if I forsake it. Let me leave the work, and my doom is sealed. I shall go through the rest of my days with a heavy heart and a burdened conscience. I feel the power of your appeals, and the power of the children's love, together with the appeal which the dear old lady [Wales] has on me and mine. But this is my life-work, the work which God has given me to do, and I feel that I cannot give it up without sinning against Him and cutting in two the line of my destiny.

How many missionaries, over the centuries, have had to battle with such thoughts: weighing up the contrary pulls of family, friends, homeland and mission field? It may be that different generations have found different answers, but never is there any clear-cut, easy solution. In this case, however, matters were decided for John. In 1880, Jeannette John had had to return to America because of ill-health and Griffith John heard that she would have to undergo surgical treatment for cancer. He travelled to be with her, and her initial improvement was such that they crossed the Atlantic, intending to return as soon as possible to China. While in America, John had heard D. L. Moody preach, and was very impressed by him. Jeannette's recovery, however, proved to be very slow, and they were eventually to stay a year in Britain.

A MISSIONARY ADDRESS

During this time, Griffith John managed to deliver many missionary addresses, appealing for financial aid and personnel for China. Wardlaw Thompson (who as Secretary of the LMS would have been present at many of them) described the impact of these speeches;

> Many who heard him will never forget the impression produced by his powerful addresses. The combination of clear statement of facts, telling illustrations, strong argument and eloquent and fervent appeal revealed him as a true orator of high order. It was, however, not the oratory that affected men so much as the conviction his words carried of absolute sincerity and of whole-hearted and intense

Home again (1880)

consecration to missionary work as the most urgent and the noblest service on earth.

Thompson then includes an example of one of these speeches. It was delivered at the Jubilee meetings of the Congregational Union of England and Wales, in Manchester, in October 1881. The following extracts give a sense of the occasion and provide a review, from Griffith John's own standpoint, of his thirty years' labours in China:

> The treaty of 1842 began to open the country to merchants and missionaries ... I mention the missionary, not because he was thought of by the plenipotentiaries at that time, but because I see in that event the finger of God, and a Divine purpose infinitely superior to that of saturating China with opium, or even British manufactures ...
>
> When I arrived in 1855 there were only five spots in the whole Empire at which the missionary could pitch his tent. The vast interior was closed against him. He might go wherever he pleased, but he must be back within twenty-four hours. It was the treaty of 1860 that opened China; and it is during the last ten or twenty years that our work has succeeded in that Empire at all ... at the present time, there is only one province whose capital is closed against us—Hunan ...
>
> This, I say, is God's doing, and it is marvellous in our sight. And what are the voices that we hear at this time? I do not know what voices you hear; but I do know the voices that we ought to hear. In the first place we ought to hear that Voice from yonder throne, high and lifted up—the voice of God ringing in all our churches and saying, "Whom shall I send, and who will go for us?" and from these churches we ought

to hear 10,000 voices rising in gladsome response, saying, "Here am I; send me" ...

Then there is another point which I wish to bring before you, and that is that the Gospel of Jesus Christ is the great need of China. Buddhism and Taoism can make the people superstitious, but not religious. The tendency of Confucianism has been to dry up the religious faith of the nation, and to make it the most unspiritual thing imaginable ... and hence I plead here most earnestly for China, that you send missionaries out to China—your very best men—to make known the glad tidings of salvation, because in my heart I believe that the regeneration of China depends upon it ...

We want ... your best men. We want able-bodied men, because there is a great deal of physical work to be done in China. We want able-souled men. You must not send us to China, nor, I believe, to any other part of the heathen world, inferior men. We want men with the three G's at least—grace, gumption, and grit. A graceless man as a missionary is a pitiful thing to behold; but I have almost more hope of a graceless man to begin with than of a man without common sense; for ... if a man has no grace, he can get it for the asking, but if he does not bring common sense with him into the world, he cannot get it at all ...

We do not want John Bulls; we do not want Taffys ... we do not want men to go to China and say, "I am an Englishman, or a Briton, or an American," No, we want men—many-sided men, full-orbed men, full of solar light, full of humanity, and full of the Holy Ghost ...

Do not send us into China your weaklings—men that stammer, and cannot interest an English congregation.

Home again (1880)

A man that cannot talk English will never be able to talk Chinese; and do you expect to see a man that cannot influence an English congregation move the hearts of the phlegmatic Chinese? It is utterly impossible. We must have the best men if we have any at all; and as for your inferior men, keep them for yourselves.

The particular phrase describing the essential aptitudes of a missionary—'grace, grit and gumption'—became, in the twentieth century, something of a cliché, although it has been less familiar in recent years. It is interesting to note its origin. Although used here by Griffith John in a missionary address of 1882, he had coined the phrase many years before, when learning his trade in Shanghai in 1858.

In 1904, a particular financial appeal sent out from Hankou received a donation from a Baptist missionary in Shandong, with the following explanation attached:

I do [this] with peculiar pleasure, not from any special interest in the Tract Society ... but merely as a small token of veneration for the Prince of living missionaries in China. As a schoolboy aged sixteen, I heard Griffith John in 1881, and then and there I vowed I would be a missionary in China. In 1892 the vow was fulfilled, and the vow made as a boy under the influence of a single speech of Griffith John's has never been regretted. It is more than twenty-three years since I saw his face and heard his voice, but I am glad of this opportunity of showing, in however small a way, my appreciation of one who under God called me to the noblest service and the grandest mission-field in the world.

W. D. LONGSTAFF'S HYMN

Another interesting consequence of this, Griffith John's

last visit to Britain before his retirement, arose from his attendance at the Keswick Convention of 1882. He was preaching on 1 Peter 1:15: 'But as he which hath called you is holy, so be ye holy in all manner of conversation.' He was insisting on the priority that the Christian must give to being holy and on the time that should be given for such a work. He repeated often, 'Take time to be holy.' A man from Sunderland, William Dunn Longstaff, was in the congregation and was so impressed by the message that he formed John's exhortations and phrases from the sermon into a hymn. And so was born the familiar hymn:

> Take time to be holy, speak oft with your Lord;
> Abide in him always and feed on His Word.
> Make friends of God's children, help those who are weak;
> Forgetting in nothing His blessing to seek.
>
> Take time to be holy, the world rushes on;
> Spend much time in secret with Jesus alone.
> By looking to Jesus like Him you shall be;
> Your friends in your conduct, His likeness shall see.
>
> Take time to be holy, let Him be your guide:
> And run not before Him whatever betide;
> In joy and in sorrow still follow your Lord,
> And looking to Jesus, still trust in His Word.
>
> Take time to be holy, be calm in your soul;
> Each thought and each temper beneath His control.
> Thus led by His Spirit and filled with His love,
> You soon shall be fitted for service above.

Although Griffith John made such effective use of his visits to his homeland, he would never have returned had it not been for the failing health of Margaret in 1870,

Home again (1880)

and then Jeannette in 1880. His views on furloughs—periodic returns to the home country for recuperation and deputation duties—were fixed. He believed that furloughs should be avoided. They were unsettling and could make missionaries too ready to leave difficult situations. His actions confirmed his beliefs. On three occasions, in 1888, 1894 and 1906, he was invited to the Chairmanship of the Congregational Union of England and Wales for the following year. This would have involved a lengthy stay of some months in Britain. In 1906 the state of his health made acceptance impossible, but on the first two occasions he was just as certain that he had to decline. He wrote to Wardlaw Thompson, in 1888:

> I hope that you have made it impossible for my name to come up in May, for I could not possibly accept the honour, even if elected. *I cannot leave China just now ...*

He explained his position in a letter to his old Swansea pastor, Elijah Jacob:

> As to the Chair itself, I can sincerely say that it presents no attractions to me. I know the honour is great; but it is an honour that I do not covet. The work in China so completely absorbs my thoughts and affections that everything else appears to me comparatively insignificant by its side.

In 1895 he felt unable to refuse the request of the directors of his own missionary society. In their plans for the centenary celebrations of the LMS it was hoped that two or three of their best known and most widely respected workers in the field would return home to take part in the celebratory services. In the event, however, he had to withdraw his acceptance. War with Japan had produced further unrest in China:

I don't feel that I can leave these converts in the midst of the possibilities that are right before us ... I cannot bring myself to see that it would be right on my part to turn my back upon [them] at such a time as this ... Can I serve the cause of Christ, or even the interest of the Society in any better way than by watching over the Mission in Central China in the midst of this crisis?

Jeannette's death

The hopes expressed by doctors in New York and London proved delusive and Jeannette had to return to America for another operation. She was able to join her husband again in China by November 1883, but died, apparently of peritonitis, on 29 December 1885. The previous year, Mary John, then twenty years old, had returned to China to be with her father. She helped nurse her step-mother, and then looked after her father during his remaining twenty-seven years as a widower. George Sparham from Brighton had joined the LMS personnel at Hankou in 1885, and in the years following he was a constant companion to Griffith John on his itinerating journeys. In 1891, he and Mary married and Griffith John rearranged his home so that they could live with him. The sacrifices endured by her parents were to be Mary's experience also: the fierce Hankou summer claiming the life of one of her children, a baby boy. Two other boys, Griffith and Benjamin, survived. George Sparham was to become one of the leading figures in the LMS in China, serving in that country for forty-five years.

14

Revival, Hunan, and Revolution (1894–1900)

Revival

Griffith John had experienced church life in a time of revival in Swansea: first as an eight-year-old boy in 1839, and then again as a nineteen-year-old in 1850. He was to know it again in China. His own account of the period makes stirring reading. The region involved lay about a hundred miles west of Hankou. It included Hiau-Kian (Xiaogan), that district where, in 1876, he had experienced such violent opposition.

> It was in 1894 that I was, for the first time, brought face to face with this remarkable movement. In the beginning of that year our evangelist Wei Teh-sheng, who was then a colporteur, visited King-shan. As he was passing through the district he came into contact with a number of people who

seemed wonderfully prepared for his message. They had lost all faith in idolatry, and professed to have no faith in Roman Catholicism. They gave up their idols to Mr Wei and begged him to stay with them and teach them. Having spent some weeks at the place, he returned to Hankou, and gave us a report of the work such as took us all by surprise.

It was not until the next year that I was able to visit. On our arrival we were met by a large number of converts. They gave us a right royal reception, and would have killed us with kindness. Out of the multitudes who came before us we baptized only forty-five adults. We might have baptized hundreds had we been less exacting. Both Mr Bonsey and myself were surprised at the amount of knowledge the candidates possessed, and the evident sincerity which most of them evinced. The work in King-shan has been growing steadily during these four years, and we have now in that district several hundreds of baptized converts. Most of the Christians are respectable farmers and farm-labourers. A similar work is going on in the districts of Tien-men, Yun-mung, and Hiau-Kan ... On a recent visit I baptized in the Hiau-Kan district 166 persons, of whom 131 were adult believers.

Thus the fire has been spreading during these four years in a wonderful manner, and, so far as I can see at the present time, is destined to spread. The movement took me by surprise. Though I had been in China forty years I found myself unprepared for it. I could hardly believe in its reality. It seemed too good to be true. And yet this is what I had been praying for ever since I came to China.

By July 1895, he could report that all the converts baptized the previous year remained strong and firm and that there were another 190 waiting for baptism. 'About forty villages have become more or less Christian, and the work looks as if it might spread all over that part of the country ... When are you going to send us men for Ying-shan and Yun-mung on the one hand, and for Tien-men and King-shan on the other?'

In August 1896 the awakening was still continuing: '... the work is spreading rapidly in every direction around us. There are hundreds in the counties of Tien-men and King-shan asking for baptism; the next time I go there I shall baptize, in all probability, from 200 to 300 persons, the interest in the truth is wide-spread in the whole of that region.'

HUNAN—'THE LAST PROVINCE'

The first missionary journey into the hostile province of Hunan was made in 1880 by Griffith John and John Archibald of the Bible Society of Scotland. At Siantang, the rapidly gathering crowd stopped them from entering the city and on fleeing back to their boat they were attacked again, as John Archibald described:

> A loud shouting up the river claimed our attention, and there we saw bearing down upon us a number of huge ferry-boats filled with buckets of filth and crowded with men waving long-handled ladles. On they came, yelling and waving. The intention was plain enough. Had it been a case of any orthodox forms of martyrdom—the sword or the stake—I believe we might have faced it, but to be smothered in filth of such a kind that I may not describe it was too much. I sprang to the anchor chain, Dr John lent a hand in raising the sail, and in a moment we were off as fast as the wind could take us.

Another attempt was made by the two men in 1883. At the first city they visited, Lungyang, they were repulsed and attacked by the mob. Only the protection of a band of soldiers sent by the magistrate to escort them out of the city enabled them to escape to their boat.

Griffith John did not attempt to visit Hunan again for another fourteen years. Men from other societies did so, but with the same lack of success. Yet John could write, in 1891:

> I believe that Hunan is going to be opened, and that I shall be in Changsha before I die. I have prayed for this long, and I am confident God is going to answer my prayer. This I want you to look upon as settled and fixed; and I want you also to be prepared for the good time coming.

There were however Chinese Christians at Hengzhou (Hengyang), the second largest city of Hunan. These had been gathered through the witness of Wang Lieng King, who had been converted in Hankou and returned to his home. In 1897, Griffith John and George Sparham, by now his son-in-law, travelled the 400 miles by boat to the city. Showers of stones and mud from a crowd on the banks of the river again kept them from entering the city, but anchored overnight about two miles away, they met the members of the little church:

> They begged us to baptize them ... we resolved to comply with their wishes. Some time was spent in examining the candidates ... We were delighted to find how well they had been taught by Mr Wang Lien-King ... Then the rite was administered to thirteen men ... It was to us joy unspeakable to admit these thirteen men into our communion. We have many Hunan men in the Church, baptized at Hankow

and elsewhere. But these thirteen are, so far as I know, the first baptisms ever witnessed in Hunan itself—that is in connection with the Protestant Church. It was a glorious ending to a very stormy day. That day, April 6, 1897, I shall never forget, and that evening I shall never forget. If ever there has been a Bethel in this world, surely our boat was a Bethel that evening.

When John again visited the province in 1899, he could say, 'This was my fourth visit to Hunan, but the first on which I was not made to feel that my life was in danger.' They entered many cities and towns, preaching to thousands of people. 192 people were baptized during the journey: 'We might have baptized hundreds more, for there were many hundreds of candidates; but it seemed to us that we could not be too careful in regard to this matter at this initial stage of the work in Hunan.' In October of the same year, he travelled to Yochow with the purpose of obtaining premises in the city and establishing his colleague, a Mr Greig, as the first settled LMS missionary in Hunan. In 1902, Griffith John noted in a letter home, 'You know that our great work is in the Hengzhou prefecture and two of the adjoining prefectures. We have in that region 5,000 candidates for baptism at least.'

In 1899 Griffith John had written to Wardlaw Thompson:

My dreams—the dreams of years—are being fulfilled one by one. My dream of seeing a strong mission in Central China is fulfilled. My dream of carrying the Gospel from Hankou through Hunan to the borders of Canton has been fulfilled. My dream of seeing an educational institution established in connection with our Mission in Central China has been fulfilled. In three years hence the Hunan Mission will be on its feet and so will the educational institution.

So swiftly did the Hunanese attitude towards foreigners and foreign ways change that the province overtook all others in setting aside the traditional Confucian Classics examination system and setting up modern primary and secondary education. The advice of missionaries was sought and the mission schools used as models. A 2007 biography of Mao Tse-Tung describes how as a seventeen-year-old, in 1911, he began to receive a modern education:

> Mao's province, Hunan, which had some 30 million inhabitants, became one of the most liberal and exciting places in China ... Large numbers of foreign traders and missionaries arrived, bringing Western ways and institutions. By the time Mao heard about modern schools, there were over a hundred of them, more than in any other part of China, and including even a few for women.
>
> One was located near Mao ... The school was an eye-opener for Mao ...

Griffith John set up his schools as maidservants for the Christian church. He knew well enough that education on its own can never save a soul: it can only produce cleverer sinners, as the saying goes. How ironic that such an atheist as Mao should have received his intellectual quickening through a system modelled in part on the work of this gentle, loving Christian.

The Boxer uprising, 1899—1901

In 1898, the young Guang Xu, Emperor of the Qing (Manchu) dynasty, and his party of progress put forward a programme of radical and sweeping reform—the Hundred

Days' Reform. This was a modernising policy to reshape the cultural, political, social and educational structures of the country on a Western European pattern. The Emperor's senior adviser on the reforms was Kang Youwei, who had himself been greatly influenced by the writings of Timothy Richard. It was Kang Youwei's testimony: 'I owe my conversion to reform chiefly on the writings of two missionaries, the Rev. Timothy Richard and the Rev. Dr. Young J. Allen.'

However, the reform programme being implemented by the Emperor was too radical, violent and sudden for the conservative elements of the Imperial court. With their backing, the Empress Dowager Ci Xi, Guang Xu's aunt, engineered a *coup d'etat*. The emperor was put under house arrest and most of the reforms halted. This was the political background to the Boxer Uprising.

The Righteous and Harmonious Fists was a secret martial arts movement of the northern provinces. Its members held to Taoist and Buddhist beliefs involving physical and military training, prayers and incantations, spirit possession, and a claim of supernatural invulnerability to all weapons. They rebelled against the weaknesses of the ruling Qing dynasty and, particularly, against all foreign influence and innovations. Their slogan was 'Revive the Qing and destroy the foreigners.' The name 'Boxers' was first given to them by American missionaries in the north. The weak Beijing government had failed to prevent France, Japan, Russia and Germany gaining greater and greater rights and privileges within the country. This was perceived as foreign aggression and greatly swelled the ranks of the Boxers. In one complaint of the period from a local official, a familiar and longstanding grudge is expressed: 'Take away your missionaries and your opium and you will be welcome.' In the Shandong province the Boxers gained the support of the local Chinese peasantry following a drought and floods which forced farmers into the cities to look for food.

In January 1900, the Empress Dowager, seeing the advantage to her party of this anti-foreign movement, changed her policy towards the Boxers and began encouraging and defending them. In the spring of 1900, the Boxer movement spread rapidly north from Shandong into the countryside near Beijing. Boxers burned Christian churches, killed Chinese Christians, and intimidated Chinese officials who stood in their way. The European diplomats in Beijing, fearing for their lives, retreated into their Legation Quarter, setting up defensive perimeters around the compound. A long siege ensued with constant bombardment, resulting in the death or wounding of about forty percent of the legation guards. An international force of 2,000 sailors and marines led by the British Vice-Admiral Edward Seymour was sent to Beijing in June, but failed to get nearer than twenty-five kilometres from the city. It was forced to retreat and then, being ambushed, had itself to be rescued by a second expedition sent from Tientsin.

On 21 June, Empress Dowager Ci Xi declared war on all foreign powers, but the rebellion was ultimately defeated when a 50,000-strong international force drawn from six European nations together with Russia and Japan arrived on the northern coast. An armistice was declared and the Legation siege lifted in August. It was widely reported that the massacres and atrocities committed by the Allied troops as they set about establishing order in the provinces around Beijing were as bad as, if not worse than, the actions of the Boxers.

During the spring and summer months of 1900, Protestant and Catholic missionaries and their Chinese disciples were massacred throughout northern China, some by Boxers and others by government troops and authorities. In the rebellion as a whole, a total of at least 189 Protestant missionaries, 53 of their children and about 2,000 Chinese Protestants were killed, and 47 Catholic priests and nuns with 30,000 Chinese Catholics. Among the Protestant missionaries were those representing Baptist, Anglican, Lutheran, Methodist, Presbyterian and Plymouth Brethren missionary societies. Hudson Taylor's China Inland Mission, which lost 58 adult missionaries and 21 children, had the highest losses of any missionary agency that year. This was because so many of the CIM stations were situated in the north.

WHAT OF HANKOU?

The missionaries and Chinese believers in Hubei and Hunan were spared the killings and atrocities. This, under God's providence, was entirely due to the wise statesmanship of the regional governor, Zhang Zhidong. He, together with Li Hongzhang at Canton, Yuan Shikai in Shandong, and Liu Kunyi at Nanjing, commanded substantial modernized armies, but they refused to join in the Imperial Court's declaration of war and withheld the knowledge of it from the Chinese population in the south.

Zhang was one of eight viceroys in China at this time and had jurisdiction over the provinces of Hubei, Hunan and Anhui. He entered into negotiations with the Europeans in Shanghai to keep his army out of the conflict. The neutrality of these provincial and regional governors kept the majority of China out of the rebellion.

Hankou became the centre into which all the escaping missionaries from the north poured. A report written by Wardlaw Thompson at the time describes the steps taken:

> The ladies and children [of all missionaries in Hubei and Hunan] were ordered from Hankou and other places in the interior to the coast, and many missionary stations were, as a wise precaution, entirely deserted by their occupants for several months The majority of the missionaries in the interior of Northern and Western China who escaped from the fury of the Boxers found their way to safety through Central China and down to the Yang-tse valley by way of Hankou. The letters from that mission are full of a pathetic and tragic interest as they tell of the condition of those who in succession arrived.

He included in his report a letter from Griffith John, from whom he was receiving most of his information on the crisis.

August 27, 1900

Missionaries are arriving here almost every day, on their way from the interior to the coast. The tale which some of them have to tell is enough to make one's blood run cold. I have never heard anything so gruesome as the story of the suffering and barbarism which the Shan-Si [Shanxi] refugees have brought with them. Others also have sad tales to tell; but this is the saddest I have heard. There are tales that have not reached us yet, which will surpass this in horror. The Pao-ting-fu tale when told will throw every other into the shade. I am looking forward to it with absolute dread,

Revival, Hunan, and Revolution (1894–1900)

as I do that of Tai-yuen-fu ... [The *Taiyuan Massacre* took place on 9 July 9 1900, in Taiyuan, Shanxi province, when the governor of Shanxi ordered the killings of 45 Christian missionaries and of local church members, including children.]

We cannot but feel thankful to God for the peace we have been permitted to enjoy at Hankou and Wuchang. We have had our trials here. The rumours have been many, constant, and very alarming. We have been also in great perils. Last week, for instance, we were in great danger, owing to the plottings of the reformers. They had entered into collusion with the Kolao sect and the vilest vagabonds of the place, with the view of killing the officials, from the Viceroy downwards, and taking possession of these three cities. But for the vigilance and energy of the Viceroy, these three cities would have been in ashes before the end of last week. I have always had great confidence in the good intentions of our Viceroy, and this has enabled me to go on with my work here in the enjoyment of much mental peace ...

Till a fortnight ago the daily preaching was carried on regularly, and with as much energy as ever. After the attacks made on the chapels by the mob, the officials suggested that it would be advisable to suspend this branch of the work for the present. We thought it only right to meet their wishes in this matter, so there has been no daily preaching for about a fortnight ...

I am sure we have acted wisely in staying here to comfort and strengthen our native brethren. It would have been cruel to leave them whilst there was a possibility of staying with them. Had I left them when these troubles began, I could never return and preach faith and courage to them again.

> Our presence here has been most helpful to them in many ways ... The ladies and children are safe in Japan. Some of the gentlemen are there also, but most of us are here.

It is clear that the help received was mutual. In a later report, he writes:

> During these three months converts used to come to me in batches, and fill my study from the early morning down into the depths of the night. They came for comfort, guidance and help in many ways. They had wonderful tales to tell of their trials, their sufferings, and fears. Their anxiety reached its highest pitch when the ladies were ordered away by the Consul-General and the missionaries began to take their departure. It was a sad time for them, and it was a trying time to ourselves. But I shall never cease to thank God for the privilege of being here at the time. I would not have missed it for much gold. The mental peace which God gave me right through is an experience never to be forgotten. Then there was a wonderful deepening of my interest in the Christians, and an intensifying of my interest in the work itself.

The Christians did not rise above fear, and we can pardon them for that. But they did rise above cowardice. Many efforts were made to get them to recant; but, so far as I know, not a man among them, nor a woman either, proved unfaithful. Their confession of Christ was bold and uncompromising. One old woman faced the tempter and said, "You can kill me if you like, but I will never forsake Christ; I have only one life to live, I can only die once. Kill me if you like, my mind is made up." That was the front which our converts presented to the enemy during those months of trial. None of our converts in Hupeh [Hubei] were called upon to die for Christ, but many of them would have died cheerfully rather than deny their faith in him. Of this I have no doubt whatever.

After the crushing of the rebellion and the return of Beijing to some degree of normal government, the question of reparations had to be decided. The Alliance demanded payment at the cost of a tael of silver per head of population, i.e. about 450 million taels, at 4% interest. In the next 38 years, China paid 668,661,220 taels—equivalent in 2010 terms to about £30 billion. The missionary societies were asked to submit claims for loss of property and life. One or two missionaries did so with a vengeance—guiding troops through the Boxer villages in order to confiscate property. But most of the societies refused to accept any indemnity for the loss of life and made moderate claims only for damage of property. This was Griffith John's view. Hudson Taylor went even further, refusing to make any claims on behalf of the CIM in order to demonstrate the meekness and gentleness of Christ to the Chinese.

15

A DEATH AND A JUBILEE (1905)

THE DEATH OF HUDSON TAYLOR

In the February of 1905, Hudson Taylor returned to China for the last time. He wished to visit the CIM stations at Henan and Hunan, the two Chinese provinces that had proved most resistant to Christianity. He sailed up the Yangzi, arriving at Griffith John's home in April. The fellowship of the two friends was sweet as they reminisced of fifty years of mutual love, respect and cooperation since they first met in Shanghai. W. A. P. Martin, also a China veteran of over fifty years, came over from Wuchang to join them. A famous photograph exists of the three bearded men, the two guests seated and Griffith John standing, on the veranda of his home. On 1 May, Hudson Taylor, together with his son, Howard, and daughter-in-law, Geraldine, departed on a train to visit many of the CIM stations in Henan. They returned to Hankou on 26 May, intending to proceed after a few days of rest to Changsha, Hunan, by boat. A. J. Broomhall describes this, the last meeting of the two friends:

> Griffith John in particular seemed drawn to his old friend. Their attachment had always been at a deeply spiritual level, and but for his mission's insistence on a different strategy, he also would have been a trail-blazer. In the event he had become a model of the effective, city-based church planter and author of powerful literature in immaculate Chinese. Of Hudson Taylor he wrote, "I never felt more attached to him than I did ... before he started to Changsha. I was longing to see him again on his way to Shanghai and home."

The Taylor party arrived at Changsha on 2 June. On Saturday evening, 4 June 1905, exhausted by travelling, Hudson Taylor rested on his bed. While listening to his daughter-in-law's conversation, he drew a quick breath, gave a gasp, and died. When he heard the news, Griffith John wrote immediately to Geraldine: 'I was longing to see him again ... What a wonderful life your father's life has been! What a work God has enabled him to do! ... Eternity alone can show how much China owes to Hudson Taylor.'

JUBILEE

Three months later, on 24 September 1905, Griffith John completed his Jubilee—fifty years of service in China. His LMS colleagues arranged a celebratory meeting at which missionary friends from many societies took part. But the greatest thanksgiving was provided by the Chinese churches of Hubei and Hunan. An enormous pavilion was erected and about two thousand people gathered. Delegates, or letters, from thirty-one counties in the two provinces expressed the thanks of the churches to the man who had brought the gospel to them. The very many

A death and a Jubilee (1905)

scrolls presented to him by the individual churches were a sign of their love and respect for him. (He brought many of these scrolls back to Britain with him. Many were given to Swansea Museum, and one is displayed in Ebenezer Chapel, Swansea.) Time and again in the celebratory meetings the same tribute was heard: 'He has loved us.'

In 1906 he wrote a brief summary of his work in Hubei and Hunan:

> In 1862 the infant church was constituted. By the end of the year there were eleven converts. A small beginning certainly, but the earnest of greater things to come. There has never been a year since with so small a record. As the work extended into the district, the numbers in the Chinese community have steadily and in recent years have rapidly increased. The baptisms last year (1905) in Hankou, and in the wide district which regards Hankou as its centre, numbered hundreds, and the membership of the Church has grown to about 6,500.

16
THE LAST YEARS (1902–12)

KULING (LUSHAN)

In 1892, and again in 1896, Griffith John had suffered ill-health and had had to withdraw from his work. On the second occasion he had retired for some six weeks to a stone cottage that he owned on the Kuling estate in the Jiangxi province to the south-east of Hankou. In 1884, Griffith Sparham, his grandson, had been ill and Mary had taken him from Hankou to this cooler, mountainous region, south of the Yangzi River, about fifteen miles east of the port of Jiujiang. Griffith John had come to visit them and, when exploring the region, had discovered four beautiful, cool, well-watered valleys, 4,000 feet above sea level, high up on the slopes of Mount Lu. He enquired about ownership and found that 'No one owned it, no one lived there, and officials seemed to be in ignorance of its existence.' Apparently an owner was found, for he bought some land and built the cottage, giving it the Welsh name

Cwm-nant ('Valley of the stream'). This was the name of an uncle's farm in the Gower Peninsula, south Wales, which he had visited as a boy. More Europeans from Wuhan and Shanghai bought land in the vicinity and Griffith John was appointed Chairman of the Kuling Estate Trust. It was used as a place of occasional retreat during the intolerable heat of the Central China summers.

Kuling is now a village at the centre of a tourist area known as Lushan, but in 1936 it became a retreat for Chiang Kai-Shek, the leader of the Guomindang. He built a villa there and used the estate as the summer headquarters of his national government for thirteen years. Later again, in 1949, after Chiang's flight to Taiwan, Chairman Mao Tse-tung took over the villa, and Kuling became a favourite meeting place for the Central Committee of the Communist Party of China. Mao's biographers note:

> In August 1970 he opened a plenum in Lushan, the mountain of volatile clouds, where the Central Committee had met twice before, in 1959 and 1961, both times for the same goal of pushing the Programme [Mao's 'Superpower Programme' for China'] ahead ...

Here is a second example of the irony of an institution set up by the Christian Griffith John being used by the atheist Mao.

DECLINING HEALTH

From 1902 onwards, however, Griffith John's health was continually frail. He suffered from frequent severe headaches and periods of exhaustion and, in December 1905, had a slight stroke. His doctors urgently advised that both he and Charles Sparham must leave China 'as early as possible.' In March 1906, together with Mary, they travelled to America, where his sons, Griffith and David, had settled. They stayed most of the time at Griffith's home in Yonkers, New York State. From the frequent letters and periodicals he received from Britain he kept up with the current trends in theology and sent detailed letters to the LMS directors with advice on all matters to do with Hankou. He attended the Presbyterian Church in Fifth Avenue, New York, to hear Campbell Morgan of Westminster Chapel, London, preach and was delighted with the sermon, but was very troubled by what he read of the radical theology of R. J. Campbell that was gaining ground:

> I am pained to see how the great facts of the gospel, the facts on which we have been building in China, are openly called in question these days in your pulpits. And what is given as a substitute? Conjectures, bog, quick-sand. What would be the use of taking that stuff to China? Translate it into Chinese and it vanishes into thin air.

When in America, Griffith John collected together a number of his addresses: 'Most of these ... were delivered in China in the presence of missionaries and others; some, on the other hand, appeared here for the first time, never having been orally delivered.' The book, *A Voice from China*, was published in 1907. Its twelve chapters contain historical material: 'The Gospel in Hupeh [Hubei]', 'The Tract in China', for example; missionary addresses: 'The Supreme Motive in Christian Missions', 'Why do I believe in Missions?'; and sermons. One sermon emphasises again one of John's main priorities; entitled *The Source of Power*, it is based on Luke 18:1, 'And he spake a parable unto them ... that men ought always to pray, and not to faint.'

Griffith John and the Sparhams were back in Hankou before the end of 1907, but as he tried to settle into his old work it was clear that his energy and discernment were greatly curtailed. He himself said that 'I can face work to any extent' and that the problem was that 'I cannot face worry and depression.' His colleagues, however, were more objective in their diagnosis: 'The old *will* to do is as strong as ever'; 'The difficulty will be to keep Dr John from undertaking too much.' Sometimes their frustration got the better of them: 'If only he could have kept to his translation work! But he cannot do any translation work and ought not to attempt the administrative work!' On 6 October 1909, he suffered his fourth stroke. This was the worst yet, affecting his speech and his mind. His mind was beginning to wander, but his body was still strong. 'Sometimes he was back in south Wales in his father's house, or at his grave longing for him to come out.' He was away at Kuling for much of 1910. His visit there early in the year was memorable in that it was the first time he had travelled there in a chauffeur-driven motor car. The last mountainous part of the journey, however, was by the very much more familiar method of sedan chair.

In 1911 the political situation in the country changed rapidly. The Manchu Imperial dynasty was crumbling and approaching the end of its near 500-year-long rule. Griffith John, who had followed its fortunes and whose life had been caught up in its crises during Taiping rebellion, Opium wars, the Sino-Japanese War and Boxer Uprising, could not now take in what was happening. The fate of the 'Last Emperor', the boy, Puyi, who as a two-year old had been summoned to the Forbidden City in Beijing in 1908 and appointed Emperor by the dying Empress Dowager

The last years (1902–12)

Ci Xi; the rise of Sun Yat-sen, who was to become the first President of the Republic of China in 1912; all these matters of which formerly he would have been so fully aware and about which he would have formed very definite opinions, now passed him by. Fearing violence arising from the death throes of the imperial government, the LMS missionaries decided that he should be sent home to safety. On the eve of his departure from Shanghai, George Sparham wrote of him:

> Dr John is as you know suffering from senile dementia, he is now usually quiet and the delusions that so troubled him at an early stage of the trouble have now almost if not entirely ceased. He is however in a pitiable condition, and is as helpless as a baby of a few months. He cannot feed himself or attend to himself in any way whatsoever. The situation is the more difficult in that he is so heavy and also strong.

He left Shanghai on the SS *Atsuta Maru* on 17 November 1911, fifty-six years and one month after his first arrival there. When he first settled at Hankou, in 1855, the Christian church in the provinces of Hubei and Hunan numbered just three people—himself, his wife and a fellow-worker. When he finally departed Hankou in 1906, a seventy-five-year-old man, broken in mind and body, the membership of the LMS churches of the two provinces was more than 10,000.

Griffith John's last few months were spent at a nursing home in Clapton, north London. Griffith Sparham would often visit him, but the 'Boy-Preacher' of south Wales and the great orator of Central China by now had no voice of his own and could only repeat the words that his grandson said to him: 'Duw a'ch bendithio' ('God bless you'), 'Da bo'ch chi' ('Goodbye'). He died on 26 July 1912. His coffin was taken by train to Swansea, and from the station vast crowds accompanied it, firstly to Ebenezer Chapel, where the funeral service was held, and then to Sketty Cemetery, where he was buried. The gravestone commemorates: 'The Reverend Griffith John D.D. who for more than fifty years laboured as a missionary among the Chinese people.' Three verses are added, one in English (Hebrews 13:8: 'Jesus Christ the same yesterday, and to day, and for ever') and two in Welsh (Romans 1:16 and Galatians 6:9: 'I am not ashamed of the gospel of Christ: for it is the power of God unto salvation'; 'And let us not be weary in well doing: for in due season we shall reap, if we faint not').

17

THE FORGOTTEN MISSIONARY? HOW SHOULD GRIFFITH JOHN BE REMEMBERED?

WHY IS GRIFFITH JOHN NOT SO WELL-KNOWN?

We began this brief biography with a quotation from a report in the Western Mail at the time of Griffith John's retirement, which included the words:

> There is, however, no doubt about the reward the future holds in its palm for the memory of Dr Griffith John, the great Welsh missionary ...

We noted there that, for all his confidence, the writer was mistaken, and Griffith John's name is all but forgotten today, except in some limited circles. We need to understand why this has happened. It is due to a variety of historical events and trends of thought that have arisen in the century since his death:

1. During the last fifty-five years of his life, apart from most of 1906–07 when he was in America because of his own failing health, Griffith John left China only twice, both occasions being because of the ill-health of his wife. He was in Britain for two and a half years from 1870 onwards because of Margaret's ill-health, and he visited the USA and Britain for ten months from May 1881, hoping for a recovery in Jeannette's health. Many of the missionaries whose names are more familiar to us (David Livingstone and Hudson Taylor, for example) returned many times to their home countries, visiting churches, undertaking lecture tours, etc., and thus made a more lasting impression back home.

2. Other missionaries in China are better known because of very readable books written by them or about them. *The Small Woman*, a biography of Gladys Aylward, or *By Searching* and the other books written by Isobel Kuhn, for example, were standard reading for Christians in the second half of the twentieth century. Griffith John did provide much material for a biography/autobiography produced by his friend Wardlaw Thompson in 1906, but it is hardly easy reading and had no great circulation.

3. The histories of many missionaries are well known because of the effective literature programmes of the societies of which they were members. Societies such as the CMS, the BMS, the CIM (which became the Overseas Missionary Fellowship, the OMF, in 1953) and many others, still produce books retelling the histories of the heroes of the past. Griffith John's society, the London Missionary Society (the LMS) ceased to exist as an independent society in 1966 and had curtailed

The forgotten missionary?

its activities many years before this time. The last missionary that it sent to China, for example, arrived in the country in 1928. There was therefore no strong home base continually holding up Griffith John and the needs of China before the public. In this respect John is similar to Eric Liddell. The latter was also sent by the LMS to China (in his case in 1925), and served there for twenty years. Although he began his missionary career with so much more recognition than Griffith John, because of his achievements in athletics, how many knew of his name before 1981, when the film *Chariots of Fire* was released?

4. In his own lifetime, as might be expected, Griffith John was greatly respected by, and very well-known in the Nonconformist churches of Wales (and of Britain generally). However, in the first quarter of the twentieth century, Welsh Nonconformity was greatly affected by liberal, modernist thinking. The resulting climate of the Welsh denominations, as the twentieth century proceeded, was inimical to evangelical beliefs. It might well be that the lives and examples of the more evangelistic of their forefathers, as Griffith John most certainly was, were not brought before their congregations as often as they had been in the past. The missionary heroes of the times were represented by men like Timothy Richard, Albert Schweitzer, and Sir Wilfred Grenfell—the political, educational and medical missionaries—rather than the old-fashioned preachers of the cross of Christ.

5. Perhaps the greatest reason for the relative obscurity of Griffith John, and of many other heroic missionaries in China, is the brutal and bloody history of the country

in which they served. Griffith John had pinpointed Hankou as a centre because of its strategic importance. The Yangzi River practically traverses China from west to east and the Han River extends for hundreds of miles to the north-west. Hankou lies at the heart of the empire. In 1861 it was the largest trading centre in China. Its importance for pioneering missionary work was obvious. But for exactly the same reasons its military importance was just as significant. A large proportion of the major wars and rebellions of China have ravaged the Hubei and Hunan provinces, centred around Hankou. The Taiping rebellion in the 1860s, the Boxer Rebellion at the turn of the century, the overthrow of the Emperor in 1911, the emergence of the Guomindang under Chiang Kai-Shek in 1930; all these involved severe disruption to the Christian churches. But from the Japanese invasion in 1937, throughout the bitter fighting of the Second World War and the Civil War that followed, and up until the flight of Chiang Kai-Shek to Formosa (Taiwan) in 1949, there was almost continual warring in the region. And after this, of course, came the Communist clamp-down. The Christian churches of India, Africa, Australasia and South America, for example, have an almost continual history from their beginnings to this day, and so their founding fathers are well remembered and respected. But in China, time after time, Christian communities were wiped out, and very often the memories of those who served among them also disappeared. In the light of all this, it is remarkable that anyone in China today remembers the name of Griffith John.

In 2006, the Rev. Meirion Thomas of Newport, Wales,

visited Wuhan. There he met the pastor of the church first established by Griffith John 136 years previously. At the beginning of the twentieth century the church had been known as the Griffith John Memorial Church, but since the Communist take-over the use of Western names is disallowed and the church is now called the Glory Church. When the pastor was presented with a copy of the newly-published life of Griffith John, by Noel Gibbard, he wept. He explained to Meirion Thomas, 'You have given us back our history.' All their archives, church records and books had been destroyed by the Communists fifty-five years before.

GRIFFITH JOHN'S CHARACTER

Griffith John's life was so full of incident that much of interest has had to be omitted from this short biography. What must be attempted, however, is an appraisal of his character: the natural and spiritual elements which combined to produce a personality of such integrity, determination and industry. Much might be said of his intellectual abilities, his physical courage, his remarkable faith in God and in the gospel, his godliness and his spirituality. But whatever point in his life is focused upon, what strikes one most is his humility. An early example would be in 1853, when he first applied to the London Missionary Society. His principal at Brecon College had been asked for a testimonial, and he wrote to the LMS directors:

> Griffith John is at the head of his class. He is a strangely winning and affectionate little creature, overflowing with kindness and sociableness, and an universal favourite. He is beyond comparison the most popular preacher in Welsh we

ever heard, and many and widespread are the regrets felt at the thought that he is leaving the country ...

In intellectual power he is far, very far above the average of young men, and I believe still more so in the fervour and steadiness of his piety. More than one church has expressed a wish to have him for a minister.

Griffith John knew all this. He had sufficient self-awareness to appreciate what life in Wales might hold for one with his abilities. He knew that when he preached he had a power and an oratory that could overcome congregations. He knew how he had been used by the Holy Spirit. John Elias had been dead for only twelve years; John Jones, Tal-y-sarn, and Henry Rees were at the height of their powers. Griffith John knew that he had the potential to be one of these great preachers of Wales, a prince of the pulpit, and, indeed, at one time that had been his ambition. He knew of the prestige and respect and near adulation that might be his in the second half of nineteenth-century Nonconformist Wales.

But he turned his back on it all, and chose a land where he would be an utter novice and a complete unknown. He could not be sure that he would have there any voice at all, let alone the powerful, fluent oratory that he possessed in his homeland. Looking back, he described his experience:

It was during my stay at Brecon when I began to think seriously of the missionary work and its claims. I entered college with two desires in my mind—a higher and a lower. The higher desire was to serve man and to glorify God; the lower was the desire to become one of the great preachers of Wales.

The higher desire was there all the time and occupied, I hope, the highest place; but the lower was there also, and occupying, I am bound to say, no mean place. When, however, the missionary desire came in and took full possession of my heart, the lower desire was driven out, and driven out never to return again. That was a great victory, one of the greatest victories ever won on the arena of my heart and one for which I have never ceased to feel truly thankful to God.

Griffith John's purpose as he arrived in China in 1855 and throughout his years there until 1911 was to serve Jesus Christ and to offer the love of Christ to the Chinese. The words he wrote at the death of his great friend, Hudson Taylor, are just as applicable to himself:

He loved the Chinese with a Christ-like love ... He lived for China and he died for China ... It was impossible to come into close contact with Mr Taylor without feeling that he was not an ordinary man and that as a Christian he towered far above most men ... God and his love; Christ and his cross; the Gospel as God's *one* remedy for China and the whole world, were realities to him. His trust in God was implicit ... He lived in Christ and Christ lived in him.

His heart was full of love ... His love for the Chinese was manifest to all, and they knew it. His influence over men ... was very remarkable [due] in great measure to his kindliness of heart, his humility and self-denial. He was the servant of all ...

Both men, Griffith John and Hudson Taylor, exemplified the teaching of the apostle: 'Be ye therefore followers of God, as dear children; and walk in love, as Christ also hath loved us, and hath given himself for us an offering and a sacrifice to God for a sweet-smelling savour' (Ephesians 5:1–2).

Griffith John was a gift from God; but a gift, not for Wales or Britain, but for China. It is still the case for Wales, Britain and China that 'the harvest truly is plenteous, but the labourers are few; pray ye therefore the Lord of the harvest, that he will send forth labourers into his harvest' (Matthew 9:37–38).

Further Reading

R. Wardlaw Thompson, *Griffith John—The story of fifty years in China* (London: Religious Tract Society, 1906)

Noel Gibbard, *Griffith John—Apostle to Central China* (Bridgend: Bryntirion Press, 1998)

A. J. Broomhall, *Hudson Taylor and China's Open Century*, 7 volumes (London: Hodder and Stoughton, 1981–9)

Bob Davey, *The Power to Save—A History of the Gospel in China* (Darlington: EP Books, 2011)

Griffith John, *A Voice from China* (London: James Clarke, 1907; reprinted www.General-Books.net, 2009)